How to Control Special Needs & Regular Students: The Correct Way

"Classroom Climate Control"

By

Author: Coach Thomas Stewart B.S./M.S.

With 38 years of teaching experience—34 of which were dedicated to Special Education and Behavioral Disorders, alongside coaching three major sports—I've developed strategies to create a structured and effective classroom environment. In 1976, during the Bicentennial Year, my class was recognized as one of Ohio's top five High School Special Education Programs.

Dedication

By Coach Thomas Stewart B.S. / M.S.

This book is dedicated to the students from my many happy years of teaching the regular class, and those in all Special Education Classes are now referred to as Special Needs. One of the people in my special classes was a tall, slender boy who wore thick, horn-rimmed glasses. The *Junior High cheerleaders* asked me to chaperone a dance the following Friday after the Basketball game. I did, and that's where I first met *Darryell*. A story you should read inside if my book. If you believe in God and know what an Epiphany is, *"THEN,"* you may understand my connection with Darryell. This is a true story! The book will give you the entire story of everything that transpired from a Friday through a Monday's winter evening.

Acknowledgments

Mr. John Tesso, Coach Thomas Stewart BS.MS.

I want to thank Mr. Bill Klopfenstein, Mr. Jim Klopfenstein, and Mr. John Tesso for all their support in making art in my class possible for me to teach from grade level seven for two years and the remaining thirty-four years in High School.

The State of Ohio Department of Council of Exceptional Children recognized my class as one of the top five Special Education Programs in the 1976 Bicentennial Convention. Four of my students helped present the way our class was set up to show the people in attendance how our innovative teaching methods and inclusive learning environment contributed to student success.

Jim Bill

The "K Brothers"

About The Author

Thomas Stewart is a dedicated educator, coach, and advocate for Special Education with a remarkable 38-year teaching career, 34 years of which were devoted to teaching Special Education and students with Behavioral Disorders. Over his tenure, he developed innovative strategies to foster structured and effective classroom environments, helping students with diverse needs reach their full potential.

Stewart's journey as an educator began in 1965, and in 1969, he transitioned to Special Education, where he found his true calling. His pioneering methods led to his class being recognized as one of Ohio's top five High School Special Education Programs in 1976 during the Bicentennial Year. His dedication to inclusive learning earned him an invitation to present his program at the State of Ohio Council of Exceptional Children's 1976 Bicentennial Convention in Cleveland, Ohio, where he and four of his students showcased their classroom's success to a distinguished audience of educators and policymakers.

Beyond the classroom, Stewart has coached three major sports. He firmly believes in the power of structured discipline, individualized lesson plans, and artistic expression as tools for student motivation and behavior management. His emphasis on "Classroom Climate Control" has transformed how educators approach discipline, inclusion, and behavioral support in Special Education settings.

Stewart holds both a Bachelor's and Master's degree and has continued to influence the education sector through his writings and professional contributions. His work reflects a deep commitment to empowering students, fostering self-discipline, and advocating for effective educational policies.

Through his book, "*Classroom Climate Control,*" Stewart shares invaluable insights and real-life experiences, offering practical strategies for teachers, parents, and administrators striving to create a supportive, disciplined, and engaging learning environment.

Letter from the Author

Dear Reader,

Throughout my years working with students with behavioral disorders, one thing has become clear: patterns matter. Identifying these patterns early can mean the difference between chaos and control, frustration and understanding.

Below is a behavior pattern I've observed over time. Recognizing these tendencies is the first step to classroom climate control. Let's begin this journey together."

BEHAVIOR PATTERNS
What is a sociopathic personality?

1. THE PERSON IS IMPULSIVE AND NEEDS AN INSTANT RESPONSE TO THEIR FEELINGS.

2. THE PERSON IS SENSITIVE, STUBBORN, DISTRUSTFUL, DECEITFUL, AND SHAMELESS.

3. THERE IS A LACK OF CONSCIENCE OR AFFECTION. THE PERSON IS UNGRATEFUL AND EXPLOSIVE.

4. THE PERSON IS UNABLE TO LEARN FROM EXPERIENCE OR PUNISHMENT. THEY REQUIRE IMMEDIATE GRATIFICATION WITH NO CONCERN OR FEELINGS FOR OTHERS. * A KEYNOTE TO REMEMBER!

THE INTENSITY AND FREQUENCY OF BEHAVIOR INDICATE CHARACTERISTICS OF HOSTILE BEHAVIOR PATTERNS, NAME-CALLING, SWEARING, RESENTMENT OF AUTHORITY, GRUDGE-TALK, PUSHING, KICKING, AND THROWING THINGS.

5. THE PERSON IS PREOCUPIED WITH THEIR FEELINGS AND HAS LITTLE INTEREST IN THE OUTSIDE STIMULUS. THEY MAY TRY TO MANIPULATE OTHERS INTO THEIR BEHAVIOR PATTERN FOR SUPPORT.

COACHES POINT:

DO YOU HAVE CLASS CONTROL YET?

WE'RE NOT FINISHED! DO YOU HAVE CLASS CONTROL--N-O-O??

H-M-M-M! -- "THE PARTS THAT YOU DON'T KNOW" SHOULD BE

FOUND INSIDE MY BOOK

Author: Coach Thomas Stewart B.S. /M.S.

"Classroom Climate Control"

FOR STUDENTS & CHILDREN WITH BEHAVIOR DISORDERS.

Author: Thomas J. Stewart B.S. /M.S.

All artwork and pictures are made by the students

Contents

Introduction

In my class, Smitty "Would not ask me, "WHY!"- - - He would look at the points on his chart and then begin working. [1]

You'll find out the reason! A Classroom Method for Teachers That Works to Control Unruly Students and Severe Behavior Students. The purpose of the teacher is to help the person learn to become a productive student and a responsible adult and parent in their future life.

"CLASSROOM CLIMATE CONTROL" is a method of teaching that will reduce the disruption within your classroom. It will also help the student become friendlier with the students around him.

H.S

Barb *Herman* *Allen* *Barb*

---

[1] *(See Chapter Eleven, Part One, page 64, for more details.)*

Darryell   Kim   Kim   Linda

Sandy   Cathy   Roger   Dale

NOTE: A special education teacher must have the heart and eyes to see inside a disabled student's thoughts.

You get to know the student's daily behavior, and at times, you have to intercede to prevent a classroom disruption from happening between two students. Sometimes, the "tiff" between the two students has been forgotten by the end of the day. But you ask yourself, what could have happened to set one or both of them off? That's what you keep in your mind as you drive home, and it's still there for the evening and overnight! That's why special education teachers are not supposed to go to sleep at night! You spend enough time telling yourself, *"What Can I Do for Classroom Control?"*

I have been told that after ten years of teaching Special Education, seventy-five percent of the teachers quit because of the pressure from S.B.D. OR, severe behavior disorder. Well, let's see! Did it take over fifty years for the socialists in political office to figure out that something is wrong with our system on the State and Federal Levels?

In 1969, we had students who were just as defiant and misbehaved as any student today. I would suggest that over time, today's parents and grandparents grew up just about during the Woodstock "generation" and of the Folk Groups singing and the Love-Child Generation!! Thanks to the Socialist and Political Attorneys who slowly made the changes when most of the discipline we had in schools started to disappear! From Public Schools to mostly State Schools. At one point, the U.S.A. did not have a Federal Department of Education.

The government helped the schools by giving money to start special education departments in public schools. When I first started teaching special education, I received thirteen hundred dollars to purchase supplies for my class. In today's generation, the Federal and State governments have added more rules for schools and students. I understand the federal government even has lesson plans for teachers to follow instead of making their own.

The National Association of School Psychologists has printed the following:

"Effective school discipline is critical to promoting students' successful learning and well-being. Effective practices ensure the safety and dignity of all students and staff, preserve the integrity of the learning environment, and address the cause of a student's misbehavior to improve Positive behavioral skills and long-term outcomes."

(DOES THAT SOUND LIKE GOING BACK FIFTY YEARS AND STARTING EDUCATION OVER?)

I wonder if that was said by a group of school psychologists who never spent a day inside a Special Education Classroom.

I don't always agree with school psychologists because they think they know so much more than most teachers. Well, my Master's Degree at Xavier was ninety percent in Psychology. All I needed was one "Clinical Psychology" class, and I could have hung out a shingle-like many Psychologists do, but maybe we can get discipline back into schools so the teacher's hands won't be tied so much. The teachers should be permitted to handle discipline in their classes. It is not always just sending the problem to the principal!

LOOK AT: *"Classroom Climate Control" In my Book, other "TIPS & TRICKS" can help teachers or parents do a better job without calling an "Emergency Squad" to handle their upcoming burnout.*

**NOTE to Teachers: *Excellence is NOT a skill but an ATTITUDE!"*

As a teacher or a parent, you must be fair and consistent with your child or student. I don't believe in debating with a student. Now, a psychologist may disagree with me on that point, but that's to be expected from a professional who would give a person causing a disturbance in the home or during a class. All I have to do in my class is to walk over to a chart and tell the student, if this continues, you will lose ten points. And continue with your lesson. You can find more about my discipline in the first part of my book. My control method promotes the clarity of my rules, which are explained to the students at the beginning of the year.

The chapter on defiance and class disruption raises other points about transforming a defiant person into a caring, helpful student.

Made by my students as part of our American Heritage program, we made it for our invitation to show the audience at the State 1976 Bicentennial Convention we were invited to in Cleveland, Ohio.

The State of Ohio also asked me to give a Presentation of my class by the "State of Ohio Council of Exceptional Children" at the 1976 Bicentennial Convention in Cleveland, Ohio. I took four of my students with me. My class put together a video and audio filmstrip presentation of our class for approximately 3,000 teachers, principals, and superintendents in attendance. State Educational Officials were also in attendance. *(See Chapter Seventeen.)*

Here are a few samples of students' artwork in grades seven through twelve.

There are Samples Of students' artwork. As you review my book, look at the faces and see if you can tell Student Pride! When you see it, the students look so happy.

I'm sure that every Special Education teacher would handle this situation differently in today's system. Throughout my book, I use a "common-sense" method of teaching and handling students with severe methods. I also use art and Wood-burning.

To win over students who are reluctant to participate in class climate control.

Who would be interested in my book? Parents, Teachers. State and Federal Personnel who helped develop the present-day system and anyone else concerned about Special Need Students in today's school system when they found out about our class award from the state.

Author: As a young teacher, I worked very hard to prepare every class for every student's lesson plan. If a teacher is ready for each student properly, you will find less misbehavior among the students in class. Very rarely did I have to send a student to the office for a problem with delinquency. The only times I would send any student to the office was if I caught a student smoking in the boy's restroom. A student caught bullying another student in my classroom was scarce, and I handled it with my point system.

At this point, I have four years of regular education behind me: two in High School and two in Junior High.

NOTE** I've learned that students will forget what you say, and students will forget what you may have done. But students will never forget how you made them feel.

In 1965, I began my calling as a teacher. In 1969, for the remainder of my teaching career, I followed my dream of teaching Special Education and Coaching come true because of a seventh-grade boy named Darryell Carroll (Read Chapter eight). Darryell, as a seventh grader, changed my life at a Junior High dance on a Friday evening.

You will read about an Epiphany I had over the weekend. (It's a true story!)

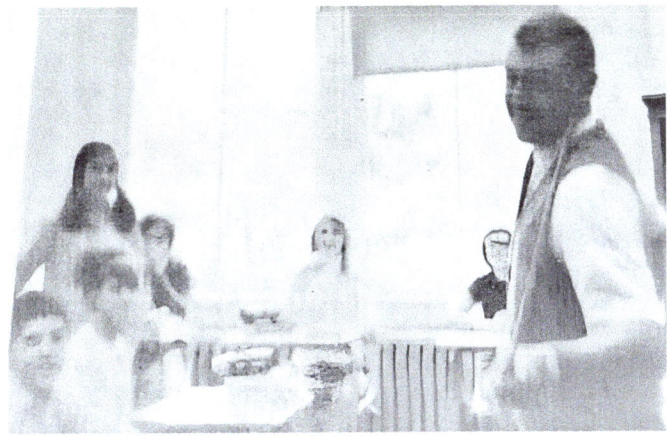

My first year of 7th and 8th grade Special Education

Four of my students are helping me prepare for a Track Meet. (1978)

Looking back at the students in the pictures, I must be proud of their accomplishments. They initially had a rough time, but they are all in their fifties and sixties. They own a home and a car or two. They are married and raising children. Many of the people who wanted full inclusion were saying that this would never happen! That they would learn better from students in regular classes with full inclusion. (I disagree with their thinking!)

The younger students made a few smaller projects on a work table. The students sold them to earn money for the class. If the students earn the points, we will take field trips to various historical places in Ohio, including the Cleveland Museum of Art and the Dayton Wright Patterson Air Force Museum.

** NOTE: *I cannot imagine how the mind of a student grows without a Teacher there to help feed it!*

** *NOTE*: In sports, what we are is God's gift to us. What we become is our gift to God.

The students wanted to rebel against the school's dress code and discipline. The parents backed many of the students and their free ideas. School Boards would give in because they feared the lawyers and going to court. As a Head Coach of three sports over my coaching career, the students in the sports I was coaching had to dress according to a code they had when they went out for any sport in our school. By the 1970s, the dress and the school's discipline codes had changed. The State of Ohio started making changes as well.

Now, the Federal Government wants to socialize education in the United States even more with additional testing. Not all students nor teachers are made the same. There are those students who can handle the extra testing and those who can't! The same goes for teachers! You have teachers who have the State and Federal laws to follow, no matter if the rules are helpful or worthless. In today's world of Special Education, a student who has multiple handicaps is handled the same way as they were handled when I was teaching over 50 years ago. The only difference between the 1970s and now is that when I had a student in my class, I was responsible for the student's learning and knew everything about every student

I had. I used the money I was furnished and set up a program that the State of Ohio saw and said it was one of the top six High School Programs in the State of Ohio. You will also find letters of congratulations from State Administrators and other letters of congratulations to my class and me.

For over fifty years, the special interest groups in education, both State and Federal, have been taking more and more of the Federal Flow-through money intended to build special education programs for each school has been taking the money and keep using it until there is no money to speak of the special education programs around the nation. They have even closed many of the special education schools down, placed students with Down syndrome into regular classes, and expect the teachers to handle all forms of Special Education with multiple needs.

Later in my book, I will have more to say about Socialism and its shifting ideas in education.

Made by 7th grade student in a candy lid. 1970.

Prologue

State of Ohio Special Recognition of the Work-Study Class of 1976

Bicentennial Year for the State Council of Exceptional Children

Inside my book, you will find a group of ideas that helped me teach each student respectfully and receive respect from most students. I started teaching high school Biology and coached basketball & track in Serena, Illinois. Then I moved back to Ohio, to Col. Crawford, H. S., where I was the Swimming Instructor for the H.S. and Jr. H. School. From that point, I moved to Crestline, Ohio, where I taught Jr. High Earth Science and was a Track, Cross Country Coach, and Basketball Coach. The Earth Science class was called a Target Class, and the classes were divided into A., B., C., and D. groups.

In 1969/70, I started a Junior High Special Education Class as a new program introduced by the state of Ohio for children with special needs. Then, I moved up to the High School Special Education Program for Multi-Handicapped and severe behavioral students. The administration permitted me to change the program's name to the "E.M.R. Work Study Program."

You will find why I changed the program's name in my book. Art was critical to the program, and so was setting up my room individually for 18 to 21 students.

The State North Central Regional Manager of Special Education notified me that I had one of Ohio's top six High School Programs. The State Council of Exceptional Children wanted my class to give a program at the 1976 Bicentennial Convention in November of that year.

My program and everything about it made it a success due to how I started my school year and the goals and standards I set for each student with graphs, charts, rewards, and a fine-point system. The Government called the program" IDEA." My Program was just called. "An Individualized Program." What's In a Word?" Thanks for reading my book! Coach!

That's my nickname for my students and friends,

NOW,

Sit down & Be Still While You Read and Learn A Few Tips that may help you in your new class.

"Coaches Student Rulebook!"

In 1968, I began teaching the seventh & eighth-grade Special Education classroom the way I felt was best for the students. There were no special programs in the area at that time for grades seven through twelve in Crestline, Ohio, in Crawford County. It was a real experience to begin a new class for a junior high school special education class without books or equipment.

No one in our system had the experience in our school, but I did question our guidance counselor "Bill Rall," about testing individuals.

Bill gave me a" P.I.A.T." kit (Peabody Individual Achievement Test.) The test kit gave me grade placement for each student's academic and social areas. A student may be in the eighth grade but may only be able to understand fourth-grade work in various forms of English, such as Reading and Understanding what he reads. Spelling and Math can also be tested for grade placement levels.

So, I used my Xavier University Professors and the Longview State Hospital with its Children's Unit School in Cincinnati, Ohio. That is where I learned the most about Special Education. I also learned from studying at Bowling Green State University while pursuing my Doctorate.

Once in my classroom, I rearranged the room and removed all the chairs from their rows. Around the walls, I set up the "Coaches Rulebook," which is class rules on poster board, and hung it on the wall for all students to see. I set up charts that went along with my grade book. The students earned daily points for each excellent grade and behavior for the day. *At the end of each week, the students who earned the points received a reward!* If their grades and behavior were not up to what was expected daily, they lost points and had a chance of not receiving a reward for the week. If the students cared, most would work to receive a better grade and reward.

Foreword

SAMPLE OF: First Part of Case Study # 1. Smitty and John:

As a teacher, you need to know as much as possible about every student in class.

If this means you make a home visit to the student's residence, it will be worth the visit. As you read my book, you will be surprised by what information you will find outside the school walls!

"Damn, Smitty, Ya Did It Again!"

What's going on, John? "It's Smitty! He Keeps Farting all the time! The way he smells, I think he shit his pants!" John sits by the window on the other side of the room. I'll talk to Smitty in the back storage room and then speak with you. For the rest of the class, continue your work, and the laughing stops now, or you'll have points DEDUCTED from your chart.

Each Special Education or Regular student should be handled differently. Smitty was being laughed at and teased by the other students in class and, later in school, laughed at in the hallway. John was loud and overbearing and was one of the students teasing Smitty. I quickly took Smitty to the storage room and gave him a couple of tums to help his stomach.

Talking to Smitty taught me more about the boy's story. You will be amazed at what you discover outside the school walls.

Read the book, and you will find chapter eleven on different Student Case Studies.

You'll find out how the case of Smitty and John was handled! In my book, I use "Common Sense" as one of my methods of handling all students. You will also find out how types of art help improve your classroom behavior. Over the years, I have found that most students work well with something to look forward to. I have also found out what was helpful for each student in my classroom and outside my class. As you explore the book, Chapter 11[2] contains additional student

---

[2] *See Case 1, Chapter 11, p.69*

case studies, including this one, and demonstrates the role of common sense in managing classroom dynamics.

DATS, DA COACH!

WH-O-0-0 DAT?

ART vs DISCIPLINE OF MOST TYPES

Learning by Doing

When you introduce art into the learning process, most People Live and learn more in subjects such as Math, English, Science, Social Studies, or Foreign Languages.

Suppose I whispered in your ear that most people are Visual Learners. In that case, I'll bet that most Medical Students in Anatomy Class wish they had taken an art class when their professor tells them, "Now, class, take your pens and draw the location of the *GLENOHUMERAL JOINT* and what it's attached to!"

What does any person working with any form of Art have when working on a project that they enjoy?

"Self-pride, confidence, self-discipline, and sometimes a smile, which a teacher is always glad to see."

You will see more information about Art later on in the book.

Behavioral control in the classroom hinges on understanding the emotional and instinct-driven aspects of human nature. The human control system encompasses basic drives such as food, aggression, and immediate gratification. Morality and discipline are learned behaviors shaped through interactions with the environment.

Effective classroom management involves addressing these fundamental drives while fostering conscious thought, perception, and self-discipline. As a teacher, using art as a tool for "Classroom Climate Control" can be a game-changer for both new and experienced educators.

BY THE WAY, as you read through the book, look at the pictures and see if you can tell me which student had a severe behavior problem at one point in their life. He was an eighth grader in 1968-1969 and brought a small pocket knife to class!

They are controlling Behavior and Helpful Hints, using Art for the "Classroom Climate.

Control" for a teacher new to teaching regular or special classes. They told me that inclusion is the term used in today's Education.

ART: "THE NEW TEACHER'S EMERGENCY SQUAD."

WOOD-BURNING BY 9TH GRADE STUDENT

Student Artwork can bring much-needed relief to a classroom, give teachers pride in doing an excellent job with the students, and help control unwanted behavior.

If you are new to teaching, my book may offer simple suggestions for solving many problems.

Artwork and Reports made by students in 9th through 12th Grades

Author: Coach Thomas Stewart, B.S/M.S

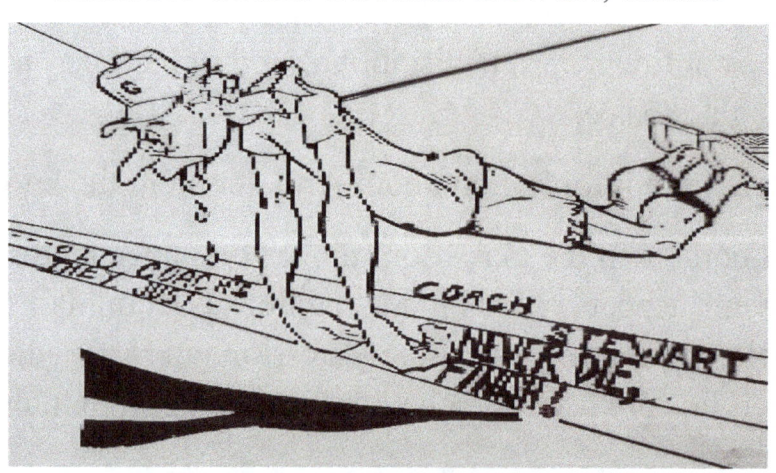

Note: Old Coaches Never Die, They Just Finish!

I encourage track and other sports for both Boys and Girls

Made by students in 1976 to prepare for a State Convention in Cleveland, Ohio.

Students Making Cider to Earn Money for CLASS.

Many educators wonder where we are today; many changes have been made in school discipline!

The knowledge a student gains from a field trip is not just incidental but a crucial part of their learning journey, especially in collaborative work. Here is a group That Worked together in 1974 to make apple cider and sell it to the people of Crestline, Ohio. We made over 125 gallons and sold it for $1.00 per gallon for our class project. The farm belonged to Mr. Thomas Arter—a close friend of mine.

What is learning?

Learning is not a passive process but an active interaction between a student and the specific features of their environment. The environment attracts their attention, and they react to these features, thereby learning.

Roy Barler and his Pioneer Research. Our Craft and Wood-Burning Projects are for Sale

The students worked on their projects if their grades and point system were average and their Behavior was average on the point system.

We don't expect everyone to be perfect, but they know the rules, and I expect all students to follow them; for the most part, they did!

Teachers in An Educational Program should provide the essential experience to which the student has not been exposed. Also, these kinds of experiences are likely to produce the desired educational objectives. The teacher must be able to stimulate environmental situations that will evolve the desired learning behavior.

Back Again Master Stewart?

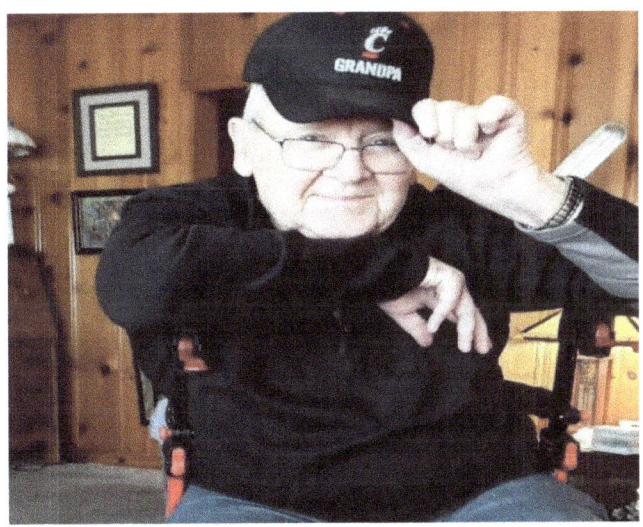

You better have a sense of humor!

Student-made projects from Crestline High School's Special Education programs.

A picture of Schoenbrunn, the first school in Ohio Territory at Goshen Twp in 1777, making it the first Christian settlement in Ohio Territory. The village is near New Philadelphia, Ohio. It was abandoned during the American Revolution but resettled in ----- 1804. Today, the site is Schoenbrunn Village.

ALSO HAVE MORE ABOUT "What is learning, later on, in my Book?"[3] Learning is the interaction between a person and their external conditions. This means that students are active participants in their environment.

---

[3] *(Check at the very end)*

10 YEARS

OF TEACHING

AFTER 10 YEARS

OF TEACHING

In 1972, I placed a dyslexic student in this math class. He received a "C" plus average, and we called it "Mainstreaming" during the earlier generations. Today, we refer to the name as "Inclusion!"

Student Projects

EVERYTHING MADE BY STUDENTS

What Used To Be Called Mainstream Math CLASS

HUMAN CONTROL

While reading my book, you will find techniques, skills, and classroom programming for regular students and students with unique problems. One of the approaches will be for handling students with severe disability and students with multiple handicap issues. However, this knowledge transfer for handling these disturbed youngsters will be apparent, as the difference is in degree, not kind! "The basic machinery used in behavioral control is the same in everyone," and "classroom programming" is for all regular students and students with unique problems. "One of the approaches will be for handling students with severe disability and students with multiple issues. However, this knowledge transfer for handling these disturbed youngsters will be apparent."

NOTE: *"The Difference is in the Degree, not the Kind!"*

REMEMBER------------------*What's below?*

"The basic machinery used in behavioral control is the same for everyone."

The Human Control System, as I refer to it, is the collective name for all our primitive, biological, and aggressive impulses. It represents the emotional instinct-driven part of our personality. This understanding is crucial for effective classroom management, as it helps us recognize and address the basic drives such as food, sex, aggressiveness, and the gaining of immediate goals set by our loves and hates. It's important to note that morality and discipline are not part of this level of our personality. Our ego is that of our personality that deals with our environment through conscious perception, thought, feelings, and actions. It is the consciously controlling portion of our personality.

Later in my book, regardless of your age, I will introduce you to forms of art that every generation can enjoy using and earning a few extra dollars from selling our product. Many people were surprised by a few of the projects that the Students made for sale.

Indian Maids are made with colored sand on poster board.

Two students, Richard and Greg, made the Chessboard & pieces.

Being able to show people and explain how they make projects is more than what many educators believe they are expected to achieve. This is why many so-called" State and Federal" officials are wrong in what they write about Partial or Full Inclusion. They say," trash like," Oh, they can learn from the other students!" All they need is a "Good" teacher!"[4] to understand what I mean about being a good teacher.

My Sample Rules By - - Coach Stewart[5]

I Don't Just Teach, I Reach, - - - "OUT!" (TO EVERY STUDENT)

I reach out to help every student overcome every disability they may have had! The students and I always worked together to develop lesson plans for each subject they had for that school year. The students were graded on what they accomplished NOT, compared to what the rest of the class accomplished. I started teaching Junior High Special Education in 1969 and High School Special Education in 1971. These are part of the class rules I set up when I began teaching at the High School Level. I also had permission to change the name to the "High School Work-Study Program."

Author: Thomas Stewart B.S/M.S.

---

[4] *(Read Chapters 19 and 20!)*

[5] *(See chapter 4 for the RULES)*

Chapter One
Why Are So Many Schools Closing Their Special Education Programs?

I have seen and heard of many special education programs being discontinued due to the opinion that "Special Education" Students SHOULD be in Regular.

In high school classes, they believe they can't function in the future when they are in a particular class! When I hear this nonsense spread around, I get very angry with the people who have spread this nonsense! I get upset with those who have political connections and have started such untrue stories that I laugh and put my hands over my mouth! I then refer to them by specific names under my breath. Many people making decisions and saying this kind of untruth really should not say anything unless they are some form of socialist program trying to stir up our method of teaching in the U.S.A.

SEE SAMPLE BELOW

How aware are you of Disabilities such as Dyslexia (inability to read) and Dysgraphia (Inability to do Cursive Writing or Printing)?

DO YOU WANT TO FIND OUT?

LET'S HAVE A LITTLE FUN AND FIND OUT HOW MUCH YOU DO KNOW!

After reading the following page, you may feel a little foolish, but you'll laugh! Read the next page about being Dyslexic. (Enjoy)

"The Three Italian Bears."

This is what a Dyslexic and Dysgraphia student goes through with everything they read or write! When I read "Da Italian Bears" the first time, I found it was not easy!

(Dis'sse littettr issa for do ifa-u laicho tu follow Di spiccher wail ise spicche,)

"This a letter" is ah U

"DI TRE BERRESE"

Uans appona taim was tri berrese; mamma berre, Pappa berre a bebi berre. Live inna countei nira forresta. NAISE AUSI! Uanno dai, pappa, mamma a bebi go tooda bice, onie furghette locche di dorre.

Bai ennebai commese Goldilocchese, sci nottinghe to du butto meiche

Troble. Shi puschie olle fudde; daon di maute not leve cromme. Dan shi gossa Appesterrese enna slipse in alle beddse.

LEISI SLOBBE!

Bai enne bai commese di tri berrese, Oillesonnebronde enne sand inna

Scius. Dei garra no fudde; dei garra no bedsdse, En wara die goine due to Goldiolioliocchese?

Tro erre inna strit?? Colle Pulissemenne?

FETTE CIENZE!

Dei was Itallien Berrese, enn die sl;ippe onna florre, Goldilocchese steiderre tree unidase; itta ausenomme enguista becose die aaschr errotu meiche, Meiche di beddse saci sai, :Go to elle," ennne runne omme criane to erre mamma, Uatsiuse Uara goine do--- Go compliene sittiolle!

Written By: (Author: Mr. Anthony Di Biasio II) Coordinator Learning Resource Lakewood, Ohio.

This page showed you the seriousness of students with learning disabilities!

NOW, BACK TO BEING SERIOUS ABOUT HOW TO HANDLE EACH STUDENT PROPERLY.

Four Major Types of Special Education

While attending Xavier University in Cincinnati, Ohio, I was told that Mr. Nick Seta would be the director of my special education program. I also discovered that Mr. Seta held other impressive titles, such as the "director of Children Unit School at Longview State Hospital." He also worked with Juvenile Court Systems throughout Ohio, New York, and other states. Mr. Seta's knowledge of every field of Special Education was outstanding.

Over the years, I was taught to use, and have continued to use, individualized lesson plans and reward systems for each student. I have won special recognition from the State of Ohio Regional Office of Special Education because it was easy to administer and worked well with all students regardless of disability. The way I did it in 1970 was what the new Federal Education offices wanted the states to do in 1975 with a new program called I.D.E.A. "Individuals with Disabilities Education Act." This was to ensure that each child or student had appropriate schooling. I just called my work for each student their "Lesson Plan!"

The government had someone call it an "I.E.P." (So, what's In a Name?) Means the same damn thing!

There are four major types of special education, and each child in my book falls into one or more of the four behavior types.

Too much time is spent dwelling on the type of problem each student has, so I will only list a few that I have come across during my 35-year tenure in Special education.

PHYSICAL	BEHAVIORAL
Muscular Dystrophy	**Severe Emotional.**
Multiple Sclerosis	A.D.D./ A.D.H.D
Epilepsy	Defiance Disorder
	Chronic Asthma
DEVELOPMENTAL	**SENSORY**
Downs Syndrome	Visually Impaired
Autism	Blind
Dyslexia and Dysgraphia	Limited Hearing
	Deaf

***All the blind students went to Fairway School in Bucyrus, Ohio or the School for the Blind in Columbus, Ohio. The same applies to the Deaf.*

I have had students with most of the major types of particular education disorders in my career. Talking excessively overlooks the treatment of each defect that we encounter in that student's disorder in special education classes as well as regular courses.

Most special and regular education teachers don't have the proper training to handle many discipline problems in their classes, so what do they do? Please send them to the office so the principal can handle the problem. Elementary class teachers will have problems, and I'm sure they do a good job 85% of the time. That leaves 15% of the time teachers are looking for assistance from someone.

I don't believe anyone in high school with an IQ below 50 should be placed into regular classes! Any student with an IQ above 50, such as 55 to 80, should be tested before any form of inclusion or, as we used to call it, "Mainstreaming."

I was the person who tested my students with the P.I.A.T., so I would have an idea of which class each student should be placed in. The guidance department did all the testing in my first couple of years. Then, it came down to where I was included in the final say. You cannot be the student's teacher and do not know where a student should be placed. Hopefully, in some schools, the guidance and administrators will have enough experience to handle each student properly. I have found that many guidance departments and administrators lack the expertise to override an experienced teacher's decision. You can't stick a student's head into a computer most of the time and not have a teacher set their class climate controls with each student within each classroom. Teachers must have proper control of each student!

Chapter Two
"Parts 1" & "Part 2"

Part 1–Controlling Severe Behavior Students

(Attention Parents, You Can Also Try This at Home.)

Part 1

Different types of art projects in any subject area, such as History, English, or Science, can make the subject more enjoyable for the student. Art will help keep the students interested, and they will enjoy the project more. The information in this chapter will help each student;

- Accomplish the following areas:

- Develop self-control.

- Develop self-pride.

- Learn the subject matter.

- Learn to help others to complete a project.

When I asked the students about doing an art project, each wanted a turn at creating their own. I decided to give each student an art project to experience a positive project they wouldn't mind doing and even enjoy. This gave each student a positive way to express themselves, control their emotions, cooperate with others, and be responsible for their actions. As a result of using art in different forms, I created a more positive atmosphere within the classroom. As for the disruptive students, it became a better way for them to display self-control. Each student helped me to develop their lesson plans. We de-emphasized competition for grades.

I also found that the "teacher-student" personal relationship was more relaxed. The students started asking more questions and opening up, talking in more general conversation. I listened to the students talking openly, learning more about each of them.

I considered trying something new early in the school year that gave Bill a chance to meet David, another (S.B.H.) student, and an opportunity to help David, who was struggling with his art project.

So, I took Dave over to Bill and said, "Bill, I have a problem and need your help." This is David, who needs help drawing out his project. "You would be helping me out if you would help him finish drawing out his project." Bill agreed to help the other student. I thanked Bill and was pleased to see how well both students worked together. Bill and David became friendly enough that I could see them laughing with each other occasionally.

Part 2

School discipline has worsened since the late 1960s and early 1970s. Now, we have "Legislative Priorities," which includes the Mental Health Awareness and Improvement Act of 2013, S. 689.

A few of the school discipline problems in today's schools.

What do N.E.A. and other educational organizations say about the history of discipline?

a. WOW! Can you believe how times have changed over the past 50 years regarding schools? N.E.A. and other organizations have stated in their "2022-2023 Safe Just, and Equitable Schools policy" calls for an end to *"harsh school discipline/behavioral policies."* They also state that *"some schools rely too heavily on suspension and expulsion as disciplinary measures*, which can limit school success."

b. Another online Post points to hundreds of research studies that say students who respond poorly to problems and frustrations lack skills. These schools are actively looking to end punitive discipline, take the focus off students' behavior, and train their staff to recognize and avoid situations and bad behavior!

c. WHY should Students be disciplined?

These are the Thoughts of the following!

www.educationnext.org/to-fix-students-bad-behavior-stop-punishing-them/

Never confuse education with intelligence.

Legislative Priorities

School safety, a positive school climate, and effective discipline practices are critical components of a successful school. One of the most essential student outcomes is stopping the *"school-to-prison pipeline." We'll only list just a couple to make the point I'm making with my book.*

• Provide training and support for teachers and other school personnel.

• Ensure access to specialized instructional support personnel.

Several pieces of legislation have been introduced in the 113th Congress to address these policy priorities directly!

Part 2 of this chapter states that regarding handling discipline in 2024 schools, no School can develop its own rules unless the Federal Government makes it within its laws to do so.

Public Schools and each State Board of education used to set the rules for the schools within their State. This shows how far socialistic organizations have come in our educational system.

"N.A.S.P. stands for the National Association of Psychologists." They have many perfect ideas about discipline in schools' regular and Special education classes, or, if you include the two classes, we'll call it an inclusion class. Like all of us, they want to replace negative behavior, which applies to all students. In today's schools, the N.A.S.P. seeks to safeguard the well-being of all students and staff.

Keep the students in school and out of the Juvenile justice system and incorporate family involvement.

One of the paragraphs also tells us that, in contrast, purely punitive "get-tough" approaches such as zero-tolerance policies do not work!

They say "that it suppresses unwanted behavior temporarily while increasing negative consequences; while the robust research on the negative effects of HARSH discipline has grown exponentially in recent years, it has been known for decades."

Read what they are saying in the red part of the paragraph.

I have read this many times, and it has nothing to do with making a better classroom! "Get tough" does not mean physical; it also means being consistent as a teacher and rewarding good behavior the same way you reward wrong or unwanted behavior.

I am writing my book at a lower reading level so that many parents can understand what I'm trying to do and say to all the teachers and parents.

All teachers have many tools to prevent unwanted behavior, including bullying.

In the schools.

N.A.S.P. Safe School Improvement Act of 2013 H>R> 1199 & S.

THE N.A.S.P. Support ACT that made me SMILE is this one below:

"STUDENT Support Act, H.R. 320. Allows GRANTS to Increase the number of mental health services and provides—School psychologists, Social Workers and Counselors—to offer more Early Intervention and Prevention. Services."

Where is the money coming from to supply more people who, over the years, have created a better classroom than a good teacher? I remember a former 300-plus School Psychologist telling one seventh-grade boy, "If he got in trouble again, he was going to step on his toe!"

A School Psychologist is suitable for testing, and that's my thirty-seven-year opinion, which came to me from the State of Ohio. In my classroom or a good principal's office, consistent guidelines set by the teacher or the principal can help with behavior!

Special Education - Student Artwork that sold at an auction.

Quitting has never entered my mind!

The first Federal Department of Education was established on October 17, 1979. That's been 45 years too long. A few politicians in the United States today and in the past feel that each state should have some control over the current public schools and get rid of the Federal Department of Education. The teaching staff can handle most discipline and student behavior if the state and federal government would "untie the teachers' hands "and give them the power to do their duties! If you have problems with weak teachers and weak Lelia and her classmates in the above picture.

Rudel Chatman Project

Chapter 3
Using Art as a Classroom Behavior Control and Motivation.

I started IEPs in 1970! Using the IEP for each student and adding Art will eliminate your Behavior and Discipline problems by approximately *80%! If You Try!*

That's just my 35 years of teaching special education talking! Also, good teachers can handle the students without the teacher crying!

Throughout this book, art was used to help with "Classroom Behavior Control" for all students. I found that by using art, even the severe behavior student became more accessible to control, and eventually, the S.B.H. student fit in with the other classroom students. It could work well within group settings; each student became more at ease within a small group setting, and the artwork lessened anxiety among students in the classes. The students even helped each other more readily.

There are many good reasons to use art in your classroom, but I have five that are easy to remember and should become favorites of the person using them.

a.   Working toward an Individual Goal - *The Coach says so!*

b.   Set Curriculum vs Less Structured Setting.

c.   Develops Individual Uniqueness.

d.   Participation and Activity.

e.   Inclusion (Mainstreaming to your Advantage.

It will work! Trust the Ol' Coach!

1976, I wrote the following as part of my Class presentation for the "State of Ohio, Council of Exceptional Children."

Children Program. Part of the presentation by the four students I took to the Convention presented to the audience was "Using Art as part of the class presentation, and "Individualism Instruction" is Motivation.

Written by Thomas Stewart

1. Help develop Self-pride.

2. Helps to develop Self-initiative

3. Helps develop Cooperation. *(Wood-burning on heavy paper)*

4. Helps develop the use of Responsibility.

5. Helps develop a feeling of Self-Worth.

6. Helps develop wise use of Leisure Time. *(Field Trip to Cleveland Museum.)*

7. Helps develop communication within another group task.

8. Helps develop Creative Expression.

9. Helps develop Manual Dexterity.

***THE ABOVE 9 POINTS ARE AN IMPORTANT PART OF THE BOOK

Any teacher or parent can learn this for a start!

In 1976, the four students went with me to the Ohio State Council of Exceptional Children Convention in Cleveland, Ohio.

This was made in 1969/70 by a seventh-grader

2017 Inducted into Crestline H.S. Athletic Hall Of Fame

Chapter 4
The Rules That I Developed and Taught Daily in My Class

1965, I started teaching biology at Serena High School in Serena, Illinois. When I entered the room for the first day of school, the students stood beside their desks until I said, "Be seated!" The schools and teachers controlled the students' discipline inside their rooms. Staff members of each school could handle the discipline themselves within their classrooms. All the teachers used their method of handling discipline within their classroom.

In 1966, I moved back to Ohio to be closer to home. I taught Swimming to all students in grades seven through twelve. Colonel Crawford H.S.'s discipline was the same as Illinois's.

Some Teachers and Principals were permitted to occasionally use a paddle if a staff member felt it necessary. All the students' desks were in rows, and the teachers had their desks at the front of the room. I didn't like my room with straight rows, so one day, I had all the students put their chairs around the room and sit beside whomever they wanted to sit by. If they were talking when I was talking, I changed their chair to the front of the room. I also tried having one row of chairs facing each other down the middle of the room.

The times were changing in the United States. In 1968, a rebellion against the rules in Schools and Universities against the chance of War in Vietnam took place. The Hair of the boys was getting longer, and the dress for school challenged all the school rules about discipline and the dress code for the students. Music was changing, and students in universities and high schools were becoming much more rebellious against many of their teachers, especially the ones who used paddles. In my first few years, I used a paddle, but only with those students who were highly challenging in class.

When I started teaching Special Education at the junior high level, I changed how I handled my classroom.

In the regular classes, the students were in ability groups and competed with those in the A-group, B-group, C-group, and D-group. That eliminated the Special Education groups.

I started teaching Earth Science in the eighth grade at Crestline Exempted Village School in 1967 and Jr. H. Special Education in the 1969-70 school year. They were still swinging paddles then, but only with restrictions. I started exploring other methods of discipline to have fewer behavior problems in my classroom.

Kim McKinzie

1970-71 was my last year of teaching junior high school. After 1971, I started teaching EMR (Educable Mentally Retarded) Special Education students on the HS. Level.

Over the years, I discovered that the best way to handle students with severe behavior was to give them something they were not bored with and not for me to talk all the time. Also, each student would have their own assigned amount of work. I used the Peabody Individual Achievement Test (P.I.A.T.) to test grade level and understanding of what they read. It stopped the fight, but I also set my students up with Dos and NOTs!!

The students could tell by my expression that I was unhappy with the two boys who had squared off for a fight.

I brought the class together in the middle of the room and told the students they could sit or lie on the carpeted floor if they wanted to. A few disabled sat in the seats, but it didn't matter. They knew that something new was coming their way. I was about to give the class the new rules everyone would follow! I set up a rule system for them to follow and added a reward system for their academics and school and classroom behavior. They could win individual prizes or the prize of not doing anything for one class period. By using art and the classroom point system, the students can earn "Quality Points." That helped. If they didn't work on their academics or do their homework, they couldn't work on their project.

My Wood-burning on Heavy Paper

All the students, even the severe Behavior Disorder students, wanted to participate in their I.E.P.s. I put each student's assignments on the wall so they could see them. They could also see the poster I placed on the wall to see how many award points each student had.

Weekly Positive Points that can be awarded   **145 Total**

1. Ten points for not talking back to the teacher.

2. Ten points for not swearing or name-calling.

3. Ten Points for showing respect to others.

4. Ten Points for No Class Disruption.

5. Twenty-five Points for completed homework.

6. Ten Points for not being Tardy.

7. 5 Points for having a parental slip each time you are Tardy to school.

8. Ten Points for no Threats.

9. Ten Points for No Horseplaying.

10. Ten Points for No Loud, Excessive Noise.

11. Ten Points for Temper Tantrums.

12. Twenty-five Points for Turning in your Point Sheet.

Coach Stewart

My Room, ----- MY RULES!

Weekly Loss of Points for Unwanted Behavior

(-25)	(-50)
A. Unwanted throwing of objects.	F. Swearing & Name Calling.
B. Disruption of Class. (sliding chairs)	G. Making Threats.
C. Back-Talking with No Respect.	H. No Homework.
D. The Print Sheet was Not Turned In	I. Spitting.
E. Horse Play (Grabbing Pushing E.T.C.)	J. Tardy Up to 5 Times (to Class)

(-100)	(-50)
K. Damage to Property.	O. Temper-Tantrums
L. Fighting or Disruption of Class	P. Unexcused Absence. (after 3)
M. Unexcused Absence. (up to 3)	Q. Sent To The Office (Each Time)
N. Point Sheet not turned in (after 2 Times.)	

NAME: _____ DATE: _____ Pd_____

TOP BONUSES TO WIN

The winners determine awards. They have chosen the following:

(-100)	(-50)
1. One free Period	2. Leave school early (with Pass)
3. Work On Your Project.	4. Dinner at a Restaurant.
5. Free Food	6. Field Trip with Free Food.
7. Set in the Platform Rocker and Sleep.	8. For one Period
9. Ice Cream (Last Period).	10. Skip a Test with an (A) Grade.
11. Doughnut at Movie on Friday.	

"ALL APPROVED BY TEACHER FIRST!"

Chapter 5
Primary Outcome for My Classes

When I first started teaching special education (thanks to Darryell), I began with junior high school, and many of them switched to vocational school, which is P.J.V.S. in Shelby, Ohio. A few transferred, but many graduated from C.H.S.

The first students who graduated that I had class for six years went on to make a living to be proud of. I had one boy who was Dyslexic and Dystrophic who went on to become a building contractor and could read blueprints. His reading level was between 6th and 7th grade, which is the level of any local newspaper.

With the permission of my Administration, I convinced them to let me change the name of my class to the Work-Study Program. Many of my students went to work during their sophomore year for the last two periods, and I made out their I.E.P. with their aid. Darryell was one of my 7th-grade students, and I had Darryell for five years. I found him a job when he was in the tenth grade. Darryell transferred to P.J.V.S. (Thanks to the Crestline School Guidance Department) and has dramatically improved for me! He didn't finish Pioneer Joint Vocational School, but he did stay with one of the jobs I helped him find, and he worked for them and worked his way up to a Forman position. He also took classes on his own to be an Electrician. You'll read more later about Darryell. Two of the students had jobs erecting the Giant Electrical Power Windmills that you find all over the country.

1.   At the end of the four years with me, my students could print and write in cursive to family members and pen-pals in Europe.

2.   *Count money and make changes.*

3.   *Work with fractions, add, subtract, multiply, and divide*

a)   My assistant track coach owned a Pizza Shop. Upon request, he would bring large Pizzas to my class, and we would practice our fractions by cutting them into halves and then into eighths.

4.   *Participate in job interviews.*

a.   *Knowing how to answer appropriately for an interview.*

5.   *Eat a meal and use silverware properly and table manners.*

a.   We had a class book about all types of manners. I told the students that if they learned proper table manners, we would use our class funds (over $2,800.00 from sales.) To go out to dinner, and they could bring a date along. They had to have their parents' permission as well. I also had to have the Principal's Permission so he could get his wife. (I'm no dummy!) I also invited a couple of teachers along for those who needed a ride. I gave each student couple $40.00, and they had to pay the waitress a ten percent tip. The students had to order for their date if they brought one. I also paid for the adults who drove. If their meal exceeded the amount I gave them, they could come to me and quietly whisper, "I'm short money!"

Everyone had a good time. The class had chosen the Roadhouse in Ontario, Ohio.

6.   Be polite and clean in social situations.

a.   They learned to talk to older people, shake hands, and look the person in the eye while talking to them. I brought a few old friends into class to see how the students would handle themselves. They did well, but they did better in our room.

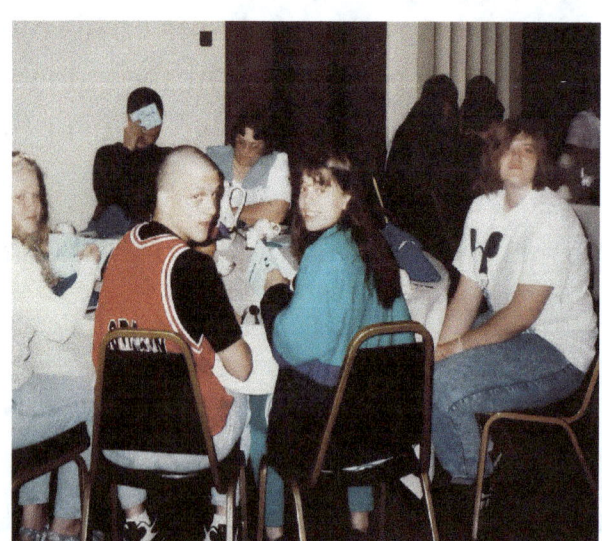

Breakfast is served in our room.

Practice dinner at Lazarus in Mansfield, Ohio

Chapter 6
Group Money Projects for My Students

You don't just teach the student setting before you; you're teaching the adult they will be!

I did just that; I taught every student the important things that matter in life, including a unit on marriage and responsibility.

The students did art projects, and we sold them to earn money for the class; at one point,

Our class bank account had over $2,000.00, which perked up the students' morale. I kept approximately $400.00 locked up in our backroom.

We used the money to eat out at different restaurants and make changes in our math class for practice. I used to leave change on a corner of my desk to see if someone would steal it. The students would tell me sternly, "To put the change in the coin box in the back room!"

The class wanted to buy a stereo for our room. I agreed to let them shop in groups of three or four, but the parents had to drive.

That coming weekend, the students were out looking for a stereo at the different stores in Mansfield, Ohio.

The three went to Sears at the Richland Mall and talked to the salesperson, who told them the stereo system cost $3,000.00, but he would let them have it for half-price. The salesperson said he was sorry, but it had been sold.

That following week, the students came into the room, and the stereo was playing my kind of music. What the students didn't know was that I knew the store manager. I told him what was going on, and he was impressed. So, he sold me the stereo for one thousand dollars and delivered it to my room on Sunday before school started.

I worked part-time for fourteen years at Sears. I set up rules for the stereo playing and the volume! The students laughed when they learned that their teacher had come up with the best buy for the Stereo.

My room was upstairs and did not have a door. Instead, it had three-tiered storage cabinets across the entrance and a four-foot entrance on each side of the storage units, separating it from the hallway. It also had a giant bulletin board on the back of the storage units.

With my rules in place, you could walk into the school from the parking lot and hear music playing. The students in the room were my students and a few of the students from the regular classes. The music was soft, not loud, and students were sitting down, many of them studying, which I felt was good for my students to see.

At one time, I had two girls from Qatar. Amy and Attaullah were not identical twins, and they were playing music that they would play at home. They were "Belly dancing" to quiet music, showing the other students how they danced at home. Their mother was a belly dance instructor and had taught her daughters. Six girls and about four boys stood in the room learning how to belly dance.

Everyone greeted me and thanked me for letting them use the stereo in the room. That went on for another three months, and we were getting close to the end of the year when Amy came up to me, crying that Attaullah had to leave for Qatar to get married. Amy would be leaving in another couple of weeks to return to Qatar for the same reason. The marriage had been arranged, and they both were broken-hearted! They loved where they were and the people there.

Their mother and dad made it a point to check them out of school and came to see me. Both girls hugged me and said their goodbyes to the other students. The mother hugged me, and the father shook my hand and thanked me for everything I had taught the girls.

With my rules in place, the music stayed soft, and my students and regular students would be in my room studying or just sitting and whispering.

Finally, I made home visits to every student in my classes. I told the parents I would like to find part-time jobs for everyone eligible by age. After school and during my planning period, I went to flower shops, hospitals, garages, and other places I thought would hire young people of various age groups.

As the students got older, I found jobs they had to drive to with their moms' and dads' OK. I had a couple of seniors who found a job at significant manufacturers such as General Motors, Timken's Roller Bearings, and P.P.G.

Manufacturing. They had all their requirements except two Credits: English Work Study, and they brought them in on Friday mornings for me to see, then went to work. They also brought in a banking account card, had to set up the account, and put fifty percent of their pay into it. At first, they didn't like the idea, but after a couple of thousand dollars started showing up in the account, they changed their minds and would put in more than I asked them to.

We continued to go out to dinner occasionally since they all enjoyed it and didn't have to pay for it. Their attitudes were changing, and they were more at ease with their manners. You can't take a group out to eat without something funny happening at least once. We went to the Roadhouse multiple times, and one of the older boys, Carl Boggs, placed his girlfriends and order. There were O-o-o's and A-h-h's when it arrived, and his eyes lit up with anticipation of what was to come! The cooks and waitresses knew what kind of group we were. Everyone was finished, and the waitress started gathering the plates, but when she began taking Carl's plate, she had it up in the air. Carl looked up at his plate and saw one bite left. He reached into the air, grabbed the plate, brought it back down to his mouth level, and spooned it into his mouth, finishing the last bite and then handing the plate back to the waitress with a smile, saying thank you!

Everyone who saw Carl's retrieval of his plate started to chuckle. Then, when Carl thought about what he had just done, he laughed, too. It was quick, sharp humor, and the group handled it like young adults. To me, they were no longer Severe Behavior Disorder students; they were young adults who had learned how to get along with each other, worked hard, and helped their classmates. But on the way home, Carl was teased for the next day. Carl didn't say anything about it; he just grinned and smiled. The students laughed when they learned their teacher created the beat buy for the Stereo.

Are you telling me that "Art, Wood-burning, and My Rules" won't change student behavior? I'll take that challenge from any state or federal school official who works with changing rules in "Special Needs or Education!" Many of today's teachers don't have the background nor the time to work with the individual students with disruptive students who are "Mainstreamed" into the same Inclusion Class." What's in a word? So, it took a young sprout of a student to come up with the term "Inclusion instead of "Mainstreamed?"45 years to think about it? Many of those young sprouts later became Administrators or Professors in Colleges or Universities.

***Mainstreamed or Inclusion, Same Thing!

***Ask any State or Federal Department of Education!

Did you notice I used the expression "State or Federal schools?" Where does most of the funding come from? There may still be a few public schools, but where does most of the funding come from? ***Will you pay for the "Partial or Full Inclusion classes in your district?" Where are all the Special Education classes? Where are all the Special Education Teachers? H-m-m-m? Try the Inclusion classes, all the equipment they use, and all the unqualified Tutors they hire to work with a student with an IQ of 50 or less! Can teachers control students with Multiple Handicaps or Severe Behavior Disorder?*** I feel sorry for the future of special education!

Are You A Good Worker?

NOTICE: *For all teachers and everyone who has ever been through a job interview*: If a Job Interviewer asks you, "Are you a good worker?" **What Is Your Reply? According to the "State Bureau of Employment, Services.**

"YES!" It is not the Right Answer!

I will tell you Your Correct Reply on Page 48.

Student Project is done on painted window glass in our room.

Proper Manners*: Always Smile and keep Eye contact with the Person doing the interview.*

Your Reply to The Question:

**** "YES, I think I am! *My parents think I am! And given the chance to work for you, I hope you will think I am a good worker."*

EXCELLENT ANSWER!

Dear Staff member,

Below are seven problems we identified at the in-service this past Friday, February 17th.

Our service has helped to make items more transparent. We will succeed if we consider these problems in all we do with our grant and school. We need everyone's help and input.

1. MOTIVATION = STAFF/STUDENT.

2. STUDENT CONDUCT.

3. SCHEDULE.

4. PARENT/ COMMUNITY INVOLVEMENT.

5. OPEN CLASSROOMS/LIBRARY

6. STAFF- DIRECT BUDGET.

7. TECHNOLOGY

Number One "MOTIVATION:" Below are a few motivational ideas that have been "time-tested."

A. Work toward individual goals.

B. Use more student participation and activity.

C. Try using a less structured setting rather than a set curriculum.

D. Arts and Crafts can help develop pride, initiative, responsibility, and a feeling of worth.

E. Planned activities help reduce disorder.

F. Promoting self-direction *(Let the students help you plan!)*

G. Put the Accent on the Positive rather than the Negative

H. Remember, "Success motivates and Praise Attracts!"

I. Be Specific, Consistent, and straightforward in your Rules!

Number Two, Student Conduct:

Staff members who are directly involved in handling students' conduct day in and day out must be ready to intervene in the student's behavior. If we, as staff members, are not prepared to help prevent undesirable actions, we are not being effective and only add to the problems we are trying to eliminate!

Much of our students' behavior (conduct) occurs because of a lack of emotional and social adjustment. If we, as Staff members, cannot understand this and control the situation, we will become less effective in handling our discipline.

The Pledge to the Flag! It should be re-installed and put back into the schools!

Our Back Storage Room With a Mini-Kitchen.
That was very thoughtful of you to say.

The answer is a little more than "YES!" It lets the personnel director know what you think

Chapter 7
My Teaching Emphasis is on each student.

Teachers should focus more on the outcome they want for each student by learning the essential goals in each student's life.

Parents are the first teachers, laying the foundation for every student's educational journey. Teachers, then, build upon this foundation, making them essential to each person's life for every position and field of study they encounter. Recognizing their role makes parents feel valued and integral to the educational process.

As a teacher, I will only speak for grades 7 through 12 and what I do to have each of them reach their goal in our society and raise the next generation. Teachers make lasting marks on each child with whom they spend time. That is why I used the I.E.P. for every student I encountered throughout my teaching career. It's one-on-one with the students and helps them reach as far as they can go without feeling frustrated from keeping up with all the other students. Recording students' grades allows the teacher to check their progress, share with the parents, and record each year they are in school.

A teacher can make the lesson plans more achievable for the students. You can give each student more meaning and practical information at the level they can understand. If you want your students to discuss topics in your class with each person taking part, give each person a part they may be interested in making and talking about. A teacher's little nudges help sometimes. Group discussions, new material, doing a project, and reading a little about the selected project help each student's learning curve.

A good teacher will encourage each student to ask each other for help with a project that is helpful to each other's project and the written page or two they may have to do to share and accompany their art project.

A good teacher will have class rules in their rooms to guide students in working independently and, with proper assistance from administrators and others, being cooperative and helpful to each other. Inclusion classes can be controlled just like any special education class can, with the proper instructions and teachers giving the instructions to the students in the appropriate setting in the room.

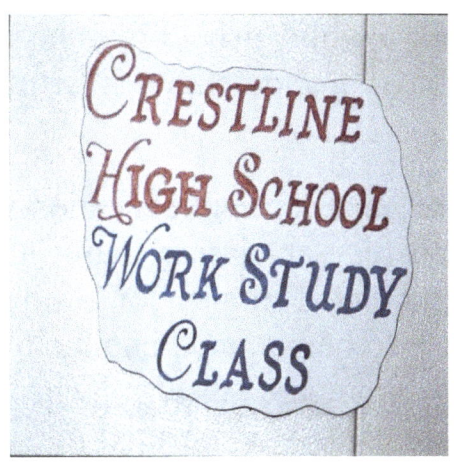

Student Projects getting
Ready for our State
C.E.C Convention. The 1776 Bicentennial Year

I start teaching students about the high school age and have them learn what employers are looking for and how to be good employees. I help all my students find part-time jobs in the 9th and 10th grades by letting them be excused from the last school periods two days per week. Sometimes, it may be three days per week if things go right. It depends on grades and behavior. They also had to put fifty percent of their wages into the bank weekly.

I knew most of the Personnel Directors in large and small companies, and they would call me and ask for a specific type of person for a job, such as they may ask for a "Black Female." After all, they had to meet a Federal Quota because they were short of Black employees and Female Employees to have government contracts. Most generally, I did! But I would tell the Director that if I help him, I want him to hire a white boy or girl with at least 20 hours per week. That would have to be a Junior or a Senior in good standing who had transportation. They would tell me they would think about it for the rest of the day and let me know tomorrow. He would also take a white girl or boy if he hired a Black female. That is not how I like doing business, but sometimes it helps find a job for someone I had difficulty finding.

For the past 45 years or more, special education students from all over the USA were being shifted into regular classes, while the special education was working with a minimum amount of money for equipment and probably many teachers that didn't know how to be prepared enough to know what to do for the opening day of school. Many unprepared teachers who lacked knowledge of how to control several behavior students were struggling with how to do classroom behavior control.

OVERHEAD PROJECTOR

This is Jerry using an overhead Projector working on a project for the 1976

Jerry and his project

STATE C.E.C. Convention. The overhead projector makes an artist out of any person who wants a winning look for their project.

When the IEP is working, the student and teacher help with an idea that the student is interested in, which makes both the student and the teacher happy. That boosts confidence in the student and motivates both the student and teacher, which also carries over to the other students.

A group of 3 Project.

I am making my classroom into a student creative area.

This room planning takes a lot off of the teacher's shoulders.

Other Educational services say that 75% of Special education teachers quit their teaching positions after ten years of experience in a mixed-class environment. Why Is That? Over time, the Teachers Teaching Teachers were using Psychological Skills and not teaching all the discipline control Skills needed to control such students with severe skills.

Chapter 8
Dedication to Darryell

8th Grade

11th Grade

An epiphany, by definition, is a moment of great revelation that usually changes your life. A sudden True Story with insight to inspire, encourage, and transform you in Divine, Inspired, Mysterious ways that you cannot believe it's happening to you. This is written from," Elise Ballard's Book about Epiphany, which is based on the experience a person can have at least one time in their life.

You are about to read about my Epiphany when you read about "Darryell Carroll."

"At the beginning of the book, you will find various ways I started finding student information and what files I used in the school to help myself. I saw how a new teacher in a new field could be on top of a new Jr. High School program and how I learned to control each student's behavior." Every teacher should have the experience I had. It changed my whole life just remembering it, and to this very day, at 83, the epiphany hit me again, and I started writing a book about how it changed my way of approaching education and my life. (Today), I'm 85, and this is the revised edition of my book.)

I was standing inside my Earth Science room on a cold winter morning when the bell outside my room rang continuously to get ready for the day's first period. Three junior high cheerleaders approached me and asked if I would escort a junior high dance this Friday evening at seven o'clock. I agreed with the girls and smiled at them as they left. (Jr. Hi, Cheerleaders can be so funny sometimes with their Giggles!)

I never realized what would happen that Friday evening, but it changed my entire life as a teacher and a coach for the rest of my life.

While chaperoning the Junior High dance, I saw a tall, young 7th-grade boy filthy from head to toe with thick dirt and mud in his hair, neck, and other body parts. Other students made fun of him, and no girl would even come close to him. I asked a girl in a high level of my Earth Science class what the boy's name was, and she told me **DARRYELL CARROLL.**

Darryell's hair was approximately 2 inches thick around his head, and his head, face, neck, and hands were all filthy with black dirt. Darryell wore a white shirt with no elbows in the long sleeves and no buttons to close the shirt, so he used safety pins to close the elbow holes and hold the shirt together.

Darryell's pants had no zipper, so he used safety pins to keep his "fly" shut. He had no belt, so he used a piece of rope to help keep his pants up. His socks had holes, and safety pins held the holes shut, trying not to show his filthy ankles. One of his shoes was split down the back, and the other had a hole in the bottom, so he used a piece of cardboard to put it inside his shoe.

I asked the girl, Dee, if she would do one fast dance with Darryell. Without hesitation or doubt, Dee said NO and started to leave! Dee was a straight "A" student, and I reminded her of her grades. "All A's, and one F on a pop quiz." I bribed Dee by telling her that if she would dance one fast dance with Darryell, I'd make the one "F" disappear. She did the one dance, and if you had seen Darryell, he would have been in heaven then.

On my way home from the dance, I could only think about the tall, dirty young boy that no one would have anything to do with him. I wanted to help Darryell but couldn't think of what to do to help him. All weekend, I was so frustrated and helpless that I cried and could not sleep at all Friday and Saturday until I was in bed Sunday evening.

I had tears in my eyes and prayed again for guidance on how to help Darryell. I had tears and was smiling simultaneously, but I didn't know why. Suddenly, I felt happy, and at the same point, I felt everything would work out fine. I couldn't explain all the feelings I was having simultaneously. I was filled with Joy and happiness and felt everything would work out for Darryell. I would give him a job working around the house for me, and then he would have money to help better himself. That Sunday evening was a great night for sleeping.

The unexplained, reverent feelings of joy and happiness came together clearly and were exciting, and I wanted to tell everyone I talked to. Some friends I've told this story to explain that I experienced what some people from church would call an epiphany: "A divine intervention from God!" I suddenly felt connected to my Creator in a way I never felt before. I knew I would meet Darryell on the school bus before school started Monday morning.

Monday morning, I arrived at school a little earlier than usual. When Darryell got off the bus, we smiled at each other, and I asked if he would be interested in working around the house for me, like mowing and weeding the flowers and garden. Darryell smiled at me and said he'd really like a job. Monday after school, he showed up ready to go.

After the meeting with Darryell, I locked my car when another teacher, Rick, yelled from his moving car and told me to wait a second. Rick handed me a brochure he had received in the mail from Xavier University in Cincinnati, Ohio. He wanted me to go to Xavier University for graduate school during the summer. They gave teachers with 3 or more years of teaching a 50% discount on tuition for the summer. I told Rick, "I don't know if they have anything I want!" The brochure's front- page reads, in big words, "NEW this summer Teaching of the Emotionally Handicapped!" I took the brochure and went into the office. I found a telephone open and enrolled in a "Teaching the Emotionally Disturbed "Class Student." (There were no cell phones in those years.) I called Xavier and registered for the new class. I was finishing talking on the telephone with Xavier when I heard the Superintendent and principal talking about a new Junior High Program in Special Education.

My heart was thumping, and I waited for the Superintendent to finish his conversation. Then I approached him and asked him about the new particular education position. I had just enrolled at Xavier University for a Special Education program, and I wanted that to be my new area of interest. The superintendent told me I could have the Special Education program in a temporary position because I don't have a degree in it yet! At that time, the first Bell rang at ten—eight, -0' Clock I Couldn't Wait to Tell People!

At about that time, the bell rang to start the first class.

I was so excited at that point in my young teaching career; you couldn't live with me! *ALL OF THIS HAPPENED BEFORE* the first bell rang to start school! From Friday night till Monday morning before School Started. Ask me if I believe in God's help! TRUE STORY! I have taught special education for over 33 years. "Check in the BOOK For Behavior Quality Control."   I believed in myself, faith, love, and everything that connects us all. "The Author, Elise Ballard," was correct; I could feel The Joy in My Heart!

Darryell was born the second child of eight children, and he is my heavenly inspiration for devoting over 35 years of my life to Special Education and students with special needs,

Thank you, Darryell, for the life-changing moments that guided my life as a teacher. Amen!

That Monday evening after school, while he was mowing my yard, my wife asked me to have Darryell stay for supper. I told Darryell we have to get cleaned up before we eat.

After Darryell got cleaned up, I gave him some of my clothing since we were close to the same size. At dinner, he looked like a new person.

"Amblyopia occurs in early childhood. When nerve pathways between the brain and the eye aren't properly stimulated, the brain favors the other eye. This includes a wandering eye that may not appear to work together or you have poor depth deception. Both eyes may be affected."

The first and second grades were challenging for Darryell, and after an extra year, a teacher finally realized that He couldn't see correctly. This had much to do with his school problems. In the third grade, Darryell started to improve but was still behind on his basic skills.

Darryell came from a humble family background. His dad would only appear to deliver ten tons of coal for his family to use in their two-story house in the winter so they wouldn't freeze, and then he would return to the bars. The first time I saw Darryell was at a junior high Dance. He would dance alone, and the girls would go another way when they saw him walk around them. Darryell was shunned by most of the other students in the Jr High School because of his filthy and ragged clothing.

When Darryell was in the upper middle grades, he was riding his bicycle on a gravel road, hitting Darryell and drug him down the road through the gravel. He had scars all over his body from the accident. The Doctor in the emergency room showed Darryell a fistful of stones they took out of Darryl's head. And the rest of his body.

When Darryell started his junior high school EMR Special Education class, he went with me as his teacher. He mowed and trimmed my yard in record time. It would take me an hour and a half, and Darryell would only take one half hour. He was dressed up. He was adequately prepared for school. Darryell walked into the room. Darryell had a wide grin on his happy face. He was adequately cleaned. Darryell still had eye problems, but by the end of his 9th grade, I had Darryell reading on a sixth-grade level, about the same level as a local newspaper. At the beginning of his tenth-grade level, I found a job for Darryell working for the city. Later, Darryell informed me that the Guidance Counselor had talked him into enrolling in the Industrial Maintenance Program at the Pioneer Joint Vocational School.

Darryell was later introduced to a young lady named Kathy, who worked there by his sister. Eventually, Darryell and Kathy married and eventually had one son.

That following August, I talked to a couple of the Pioneer students. I asked them how Darryell was doing, and they told me he quit school because he couldn't keep up with the assignments. That morning, I flew to the guidance office and found that he knew about Darryell quitting Pioneer but didn't tell me about it. The counselor didn't tell Darryell he could have returned to my class. I wrote a letter to the school board and the Ohio State,

Department of Special Education. Darryell worked at the city job and a few other jobs before finally going to the T.A.S.C.O. Manufacturing Company. The Personnel Director of T.A.S.C.O. was my next-door neighbor. He hired Darryell as a sandblaster, then promoted him to press operator and foreman.

Darryell had worked for forty-five years and only missed five days of work during that entire time. On October 9, 2023, Darryell and Kathy were married for 41 years, soon to be 42 years. The minister asked Darryell at the wedding what he liked the most about Kathy. Darryell replied, "Her cooking!" I'm sure Darryell's humor brought a few laughs.

Darryel Carroll Jr.

Chapter 9
Misguided People Writing Articles About SPECIAL NEED STUDENTS

There has been a lot of misguided trash talk about how Special Needs students cannot get along in a regular Inclusion school class, a regular sports Inclusion program, or any program in any sport. Both Darryell and Kathy worked and Retired from the T.A.S.C.O. Manufacturing Company.

As citizens of Crestline, Ohio, they paid their bills, owned their house, owned a couple of cars, and raised a son to be an outstanding athlete. Both Darryell and Kathy had planned for retirement someday. Well, being in his 70s and supporting their community like they both did. Anyone who says they can't care for themselves is only guessing what a Special Class needs! A caring teacher who will spend the time making proper I.E.P.'s for each student. I sure as hell did, and I can look back with pride at the students who made their lives what they lived and learned in school. Chapter 9 is my opinion. Here are a few short words about teachers who need to be replaced.

I'm sorry to say that, as in other professions, some administrators and teachers don't feel compassion or a need to help a student who needs it and doesn't seem to care about the student's achievements as long as they draw a paycheck!

That seems to be all that matters to those wasting time teaching in education. One teacher I remember used to control classes by crying. What a waste of time! A few students would sit and chuckle. This is an administrative problem, but she wasn't moved or replaced. That's not proper education for any student.

Students in a Health Class. Today, they call that Inclusion!

Chapter 10
Earning Trust

Students diagnosed with severe behavior disorders and multiple handicaps have to earn my trust. However, occasionally, I've had a few who would try to take advantage of one of my rules and get caught. I would smile and use an "Eye to Eye," glance at the wall, walk over, and take a few good points off their chart. I never had to say a word about the rule the student broke because they already knew, and all I would hear was an,

"A-h-h — M-a-n!!"

Trust was easy to earn. Most of my best trust in a student came over some time, such as a week or a day. Anytime they received honor points, they were happy. It was good to see a few of the rough students struggle to be good, hear an "A-h-h Y-e-s-s," and see a smile.

No matter how you look at what I'm saying, a teacher in any area of Special education must show dedication to all students. If dedication is a problem for teachers and they can't dedicate themselves to the students in a Special program, they may not belong in the special class. The students must learn that you are there for them before they trust you.

Chapter 11
Home Visits
CASE # 1 "Smitty"

I gave Smitty a couple of tums, and then we went into the storage room with a window. I could talk with Smitty so he could tell me what was happening and watch the class simultaneously.

I asked Smitty if he had anything for breakfast, and he told me, "Cabbage Soup was the only thing they had in the house to eat." I asked Smitty if he had enough money for lunch. I gave him lunch money from our class funds and then called his mother. I asked his mother if she and her husband would be home around 6:00 p.m. The mother told me that she and her husband had been separated for two weeks. I asked if it would be OK if I stopped over around 6:00 p.m., and she said yes.

Mrs. Smith told me the reason for their cabbage soup, but that was all they had because her husband had not paid child support, and she had two younger children than her son.

I found out from Mrs. Smith that her husband lived in town. I left her home and saw Mr. Smith about one mile away. I explained who I was and to step outside where we could talk.

I explained his son's situation and the embarrassment he went through and asked him to take action regarding child support. He started to hesitate, so I stopped him and told him I was going to the police department from there and calling the county child support center in Bucyrus in the morning.

My interrupting made him think I was very serious about my students and parents, who showed a lack of care.

I talked with the children's service in the morning. They helped Mrs. Smith in several ways. After school, she stopped and thanked me for my help.

This was my first year of teaching Special Education. 1969 was off to a good start!

Since leaving Illinois, I have lived and taught in Crestline, Ohio, and started teaching at the Col Crawford H.S. in North Robinson, Ohio, in the 1966-67 school year. I was hired as the aquatic instructor for grades seven through 12 and the high school boys' swimming coach, and I had two divers who finished in the top five positions of the state finals.

I started teaching Eighth-Grade Earth Science in the Crestline School System in the 1967-19 68 school year and taught for two years before entering the Junior High School Special Education Program.

I felt a calling to enter this program, and I felt that this was what I intended to do with my life for each student.

This picture was made by an 8th grader in 1970 with the overhead Projector.

I had no guidance to turn to except prayer (which got me there in the first place!)

I had eighteen students to teach and very few books and magazines to come up with from the library. So, using the dictionary and other books, I started the school year with one of the area's first Junior High Special Education programs. The administration was using the federal money I was to receive to buy supplies, and my room was being used for projectors and other larger equipment for the school library.

That first year had a wide range of multiple disabled children and a large share of students with behavior problems. At one time, I had three Epileptic students at the same time.

I used the students to help me rearrange the room so the chairs would be set around the walls of the room.

We shaped the room around and had a list of Class Rules for the students to follow and not follow to make the behavior livable within the room.

I used a P.I.A.T. Test on each student to see what grade level each one was performing. The students and I worked up a grade level for each lesson they could handle. We just called it a lesson plan. The term I.E.P. came later after the State and Government came along in 1975!

CASE # 2 — Linda

The first few months of fall were spent getting the students to work with me to raise their grades to close to where they should be. A good teacher has to know when to give the class time for fun occasionally, to do a few things to change the program of doing the same boring thing every day. I started using Art with the students on the overhead projector on thick paper or thin wood. Then, they would frame it and use it as a gift.

During my early years of teaching in 1969-70, I had a girl in class who would ask different people for money for lunch. I noticed her doing this for a few days, and then I stopped her and asked her if she had been given any money from home for lunch. She replied no. That was the last day the girl didn't have money for lunch. I worked out a deal with the head of the cafeteria for Linda to start working by handing out milk at lunchtime. Linda seemed happy with her new job. Linda dressed for school with old women's clothing on. In the 1960s, people got free clothes from churches.

No organizations by the state or federal government offered free money or any other program. Mary's grades were okay, and she was doing fine in the cafeteria. But I knew something else was going on with her clothes.

When the students were doing well in class and behaved well, they could sit anywhere they wanted. I noticed a few of the boys making a big point of sitting next to Linda. Linda was wearing a skirt with an older woman's sleeveless top that was way too big. The open part of the arm almost came down to her thin waste. I walked over to Linda's side of the room, looked down, and found out why all the boys were trying to sit next to her; Linda didn't have a bra on!

I asked Linda to take a note to the office and give it to Mrs. Conn. I then asked a couple of teachers next door to my room if they would watch my room while I went to the office. I told the secretary privately about Linda not having a bra on and with the sleeveless top she has on she was showing her,

"Ta-ta's!" Nothing more was said. She smiled at Linda and told the principal she would return after lunch. We told the principal what the situation was, and he was understanding.

Mrs. Conn had taken the girl home, fed her, and had her take a shower. The Conn family had a couple of older daughter's Secretaries.

Mrs. Conn gave Linda a few items of clothing that were no longer needed. After leaving the house, Mrs. Con took the girl to a beauty salon before returning to school. That afternoon, I could see Mrs. Conn and the girl coming down the hallway with a big smile. What a big smile she had because of a caring person.

Later that day, I stopped by a tiny camper trailer that I Lived in along with a sister, father, and uncle. I had seen this type of camper before. They are designed to be taken to a lake for temporary living quarters.

They had no telephone, so I knocked on the door to see the father. He opened the door, I introduced myself, and he invited me in. I took a glance and asked him to step outside with his brother. When he opened the door, I could see both girls changing clothes indoors.

Both the father and brother were retarded enough that they didn't see any problem living with the two daughters in such small quarters. The smell from the port-a-pot was terrible, even for outdoors.

I was upset about what the girls were going through with their father and uncle. I called Children's Services in Bucyrus, Ohio, explained the situation I just went through, and asked them to visit the home. To investigate their findings. The police were called so there would be no trouble, and Children's Service placed the two girls into a Foster Home in Galion, Ohio. I met the foster parents, and they took both girls into their Bucyrus home. I lost a student, but the two girls found a family who cared.

CASE # 3 - "Bill"

I had approximately five new Junior High students at the beginning of a new school year.

Three new students fit in with the other students and would fit into the class just fine. However, two of the five new members had multiple problems. One boy was tranquil and kept to himself. The other student was an outspoken girl who liked to start arguments with other students, which made the other students not want to be around her. She finally started doing her work and getting rewards for her behavior in class, but Bill hadn't changed much. Even after our short talks, he was still not where I wanted him to be with the class rules.

I was standing at one of the two entranceways to our room when Bill came up the Hall towards it. He had to pass in front of me to enter the room. I put my hand out, patted him on the shoulder, and said, "Good Morning, Bill." He let out a cry of pain and went to the floor on his knees. I took Bill to our Backroom; he was crying in pain. I had him sit close to where I could watch the room and talk privately with Bill. I had Bill take his jacket and unbutton his shirt. He continued crying, and after what I saw, my heart sank, and my feelings toward Bill changed. There were Cigarette burn scars on his back and shoulders with a couple of fresh ones on his shoulders. Bill begged me not to take him to the office because his dad would take it out on his mother. Latter. My anger calmed down, and I thought about handling this so no one else gets hurt. I called a close friend and neighbor on the police force; he told me he would be working that evening. I told Bob (my friend) that I wanted to stop by the house and talk to the mother first. Remember that cell phones are still a thing of the future.

I called the house and talked to the mother on the school phone. I asked to stop by for a few minutes to discuss Bill. She agreed that 6:30 would be a good time for me to stop by. I knocked on the door, and Bill's mother answered. His dad was sitting in his chair, smoking Cigarettes. I started talking about Billy and how much better he did in class. The conversation took a few minutes. Then I began to dismiss myself, looking at the mother and saying, "I'd like to ask one question if you don't mind. Billy stood beside me when I asked, "Where did these come from?" I pulled Billy's Tee shirt down from the top to show a few of the burns! She didn't say a word; she just looked at her husband. He stood up and told me that it's his choice how to discipline his boy at home, and it's none of my Fucking Business nor the school, and he started to push me towards the door. I blocked his hand as it came toward me. I looked down at Billy's feet and saw that he had shoes on. I told Billy to get in my car, NOW! The father was not going to take a swing at me, and he was too frustrated and not near my size! It was about five city blocks, and I was at the Police Station. I saw Bob; then I showed him Billy's back. Bob told me that this was the first time he'd ever seen the burn marks on a boy's back like this.

The Crestline police arrested Billy's Dad after I filed Charges against both Billy's Mother and Dad! They let Billy's mother stay at home with the kids until juvenile court in Bucyrus. The father received a five-year sentence, and the mother received a two-year probation for not reporting anything out of fear. The next day, I called the Children's Service.

Student Projects for the Convention

Student Project at the 1976 State Council of Exceptional Children's Convention.

Salish (Flathead) Indians. Northwest Coast of U.S.A

Case # 4 - "Gene"

One of the two boys who came into my room in 1973 had low grades on his P.I.A.T. score but was quiet. Her scores were second-grade in all academic levels: reading, English comprehension, spelling, math, history, and health. That's when Gene and I started setting up his lesson plans.

When we were together taking the P.I.A.T., Gene was quiet and polite with me, but I noticed a strong scent of Urine coming from him. I called the mother after school and asked if it would be all right for me to discuss Gene with her and her husband for a few minutes.

I knocked on the door, and a tiny girl of about 3 answered. She smiled and then yelled for her mother to come to the door. The door was open, and the temperature was about the low forties, but the temperature coming from the house was at least in the eighties!

The mother asked me to come in and have a seat, but after looking around, I said I didn't have time to stay long. I looked around and didn't see a dry seat. Three small little girls were walking around with diapers on, which would explain the odor on Gene. I learned from Gene that one of the girls slept in his bed with him. I talked to the mother about helping Gene with his homework, and she hung her head and told me she could not read and write. I asked her where her husband was. She replied they were divorced but sent money for the children. I wondered if she had family to leave the little girls with for a few hours. A day? She replied that if it were in the morning, she would have a sister who could help. I told her to talk to her sister and walk to school with Gene, and I would help her with her English and reading and health, which I brought in health, cleaning, and laundry, just to be polite. I also called the County Children's Health Service to visit her home.

After Gene and his mother had been in class for a while, she started to help her son, and Gene helped his mother. What was also important to notice was that the odor had gone away. Gene became a happy student, and his mother found a job to add to her income and pay for her sister. She came to the school a few periods per day to have her homework checked. Both Gene's and his mother's grades went up. They were close to the fifth grade by the end of the year.

CASE # 5 - "Carolyn"

In the 1969/70 school year, the Jr. High School main office brought a 7th-grade girl to my room and told me I had a new student with only a few paperwork from the councilor's office. I started to leave. I told the girl to find a temporary seat and went outside to see the principal and the guidance counselor. To find out what's going on. She was put in my Special E.M.R. program without any P.I.A.T. score. She is creating problems for two of her teachers. And we're not going to exhibit that type of behavior in class.

CAROLYN ALLRED

1969/70 Freshman Homecoming

I explained that the girl needed testing to be placed in my class. I followed them to the main office and was told to mind my own business. So, I told them that was fine; I'll do that. I also knew the State Director, Jay Flu-Ellen, and told him what was happening. Also, I hadn't received any of the $1,300.00 that I was supposed to start school with. They were using the money in the library for equipment.

Jay said he would be up Friday. I asked him not to announce his arrival until he arrived. Ask for me, and we'll make it right. Later that day, I asked Caroline if she wanted to return to regular classes. She grabbed my hand and said yes, please. I wondered what caused the problem in the first place. Please tell me what started the problem with the teacher. A few boys called her names, and she said the teacher and the teacher wouldn't believe her.

I told her I would do my best not to let this happen again, and she agreed to keep her promise. If she had any more problems, she should come and see me between classes or in a study hall.

I showed the State representative the girl's P.I.A.T. scores, and then the counselor told me that it didn't matter. She was causing problems in class, and they were not placing her back because she was causing too much trouble. I went to the principal's office and was told that whatever the guidance office says is correct. I finally introduced Mr. Flu-Ellen to the Principal and guidance officer. He told me that I should go back to my room. About twenty-five minutes later, the State Representative returned to my class, and I was told that my money was starting any time and the girl would be back in a regular class. The girl's reading and English were essential, but I had her promise that it wouldn't happen again, and if she were called names, I would take care of it with the teacher and in my way! I explained to Jay that the school was using my money for equipment for the library and fund.

I was soon told that Carolyn had been elected as the Freshman Homecoming attendant. She kept her word. Years later, I saw Carolyn a few times around town, and she always told me how much I meant to her and that she'd never forget what I did for her. For her and after a small chat, tell me what I have meant to her in her life; what more could I have than a compliment like that!

As a teacher, I wanted to make a difference in the lives of my Special Education students. My life was not based on the bottom- line being money. Still, rather, the productivity and creativity of my students live to see their lives become filled with enough love and caring, that they appreciate what they have through their family and God's love and his creations. And as they look back over the years be able to remember the teacher who helped make it all possible for them.

"The minds of students need places where it has never been before. Then Rearranged by God, through the hands of a caring teacher!"

Chapter 12
Using Art for Classroom Behavior Control
And Helpful Hints

The person handling disturbed students day in and day out, must be ready to intervene in their student's behavior. This intervention must be tailored not only to stop but also to prevent the occurrence of undesirable actions. It is also hoped that the techniques used are practical and beneficial.

I am going to give you a list of some OLD suggestions. They can remind you of things you want to do or try!

1.   SOMETIMES IT'S BETTER NOT TO SEE OR HEAR!

Plan to ignore or select which behavior to intervene in. A teacher cannot intervene with all of a group's irritating behaviors, so this allows students to stop their actions.

2.   USE A SIGN, SOUND, OR LOOK.

A word or motion from the teacher can provide support. A sign can stop actions such as humming or whispering.

NOTE: *"Sometimes it's better to raise an eyebrow than the roof!"*

3.   GET THEM OVER THE HUMP.

Give the student a well-known boost. Give it to a student that needs help getting over the hump that is blocking their way to a goal. That little boost may prevent anxiety in the student.

4.   IT HELPS IF YOU ARE NEAR.

Some disturbed students have less anxiety when a teacher is close by, which can mean the difference between a breakdown or a moment of calmness for the student. Sometimes, all it takes is a touch on the head or shoulder to help create that moment of control.

5.   THROW THAT CHANGE-UP!

If a teacher has talked enough, the students are bored. And if the teacher has lost eye contact, it's time for them to change gears and start a brand-new activity since the old one has gone sour. Sometimes, a brand-new activity is needed; other times, all it takes is a break. Disturbed students will act out when their situation becomes insufficient to hold their attention. As The Old Saying Goes, "*Know When to Say When!*"

Chapter 13
My Volunteer Program

As a graduate student at Xavier University in Cincinnati, Ohio, the late Professor Nick Seta ("Nick," as we lovingly called him) indicated to his students that there are four things a teacher needs to do before selecting a volunteer to work in your class to assist a student.

1.   ENLISTMENT: Determine the number of volunteers needed to create an acceptable program and how you plan to enlist their help.

2.   SCREENING: Have an oral screening process in which you determine the ability of the Volunteer to carry out a task with a student that they are assigned to. This interview is where you would assess the appearance, sincerity, physical condition, and emotional stability. If they have worked elsewhere, get references.

3.   ORIENTATION: Once the individual has passed the screening process, you can evaluate their interests and responsibilities while in your program. Their specific assignments should be clearly defined. Their conduct, appearance, personality, and conversations with the students will be observed and supervised by the teacher and, sometimes, a student's input.

4.   SUPERVISION: The following conditions produce the best results from Volunteers:

   A.   If they feel a real need for their service.

   B.   If the regular staff is friendly and accepting.

   C.   If the assigned task is within their abilities.

   D.   If they are given or have had the proper training.

   E.   If they are given recognition for their service.

   F.   If they can visualize the real task at hand.

Throughout my time using volunteers in my classroom, I could have as many as seven or as few as one. There were many great moments when multiple volunteers for one or two classes were included. Students loved it (more cookies were brought in!).

For the most part, all of the volunteers were at school for one period daily. However, I did ask a couple of volunteer ladies if they would consider staying for an extra period at different times. They said that they enjoyed what they were doing and enjoyed seeing the students, and the students enjoyed them. So that worked out well for all persons involved. The people I brought in as volunteers were mainly older retired people. They worked out well and cared about the students and the students, like most of the volunteers I selected.

Using the above criteria for selecting volunteers will create a positive classroom setting and not cost the school a penny!

Tutor with student

Chapter 14
Reasons Teachers Are Crucial for Society

The "Teachers of Tomorrow" org. has listed online why teachers are essential to society. They have twelve reasons; I will only give you six of them.

1. Teachers pass their knowledge to younger generations.

2. Teachers in developing critical thinking skills

3. Teachers boost confidence in students

4. Teachers develop Peace in Society.

5. Teachers build communities for children's growth.

6. Teachers help to pursue dreams.

Most schools today are in turmoil regarding how to handle students with disabilities or behavioral problems. As an educator in both regular and special education fields with close to 40 years of experience, I would have to smile at the teachers, administrators, and state and federal officials who have placed our nation's educational system in such turmoil because most of them are clueless as to how to reset Special Education back to where each student can come back to school at the beginning of each new year, and not have to sit next to a person that is supposed to help them "learn better." That's what they are hoping inclusion will do.

State and federal officials are willing to spend millions of taxpayers' money to prove their point. I would say that most educators making the decision have never been in a Special Needs classroom, either one set up or one set up 45 years ago! Most of the lower-ability students are lost and made to feel useless within these inclusion settings! You can't just plug a student into a computer and expect them to receive everything they need to function outside of the school and in the community! The present system is setting the student up for failure!

Some educators feel our present students are not receiving the education to do "critical thinking."

All it takes is to change how the state and federal education departments select what is best for the schools in their testing methods. The state and federal governments are at fault for their testing guidelines; "All students must meet State and Federal Standards" leads to Socialism at the highest levels. That is not how our country was founded!

Made by a student with multiple problems, he then found something he enjoyed and made a change in his life.

Chapter 15
Today's Educational Turmoil

Not all students learn at the same rate, and the state wants us to use the same guidelines for testing and passing for all students. Where are all the Public Schools today? Many politicians today feel we should abolish the Federal Department of Education. I taught for most of my career without a Federal Department of Education.

Does the word "Turmoil" cross your mind?

I consider the term "Full inclusion" to be one of the useless terms used in this more modern terminology! They are trying to date the term "inclusion" back to my generation of the 1960s and 1970s! In 1975, the NEW Federal Education Department set up a program that they thought was new, and they termed the new program "I.D.E.A.!" which stands for

"Individual Disability Education Act!" I started my individualized program in the 1970/71 school year. New school education began with President Johnson's new "War on Poverty" laws in 1965.

READ THE REPORTS:

1.   **Written by Bev Johns**: "Does Full Inclusion Violate Federal Law?"

2.   **Socialism in Education**, Written by Jacob Hornberger, February 14, 2020. "It would be virtually impossible to find A better example of socialism here in the United States than the public schooling system exists in every U.S. state.

3.   The Reason WE Learn by Deb Fillman.

As I pointed out, every writer and reporter has their own opinion. But, as a conclusion to this part of my book, *I agree with the need to cut back on the importance of the student needing as much testing as the state and federal governments seem to think there should be*! Also, let's avoid the old term "*No Child Left Behind Act of 2001*." George Bush promoted that.

It reauthorized the Elementary and Secondary Education Act and included Title One provisions for disadvantaged students. It demanded that standard-based education be set higher and that establishing measurable goals could improve individual educational outcomes. To receive federal funding, States had to create and give assessments to all students at selected grade levels!

Once upon a time, in this modern world, we live in, there was an up-scale version of education with money coming to each school system to set up the New Special Education programs with what was called "Flo-Through" money. Everything was going in a positive direction until very few politicians found that they could use part of the money by updating the Federal Department of Education and making the changes over the next generations with many changes that have affected every state in the U.S.

There are increasingly strict state and federal rules determining a student's graduation, and the Special Education class has almost completely disappeared. It was intended for students who needed extra help and had multiple problems, but that all has changed today.

According to the N.E.A. Today, in an article written by Brenda Alvarez, "We are teaching in Turmoil. Teachers are afraid of the students' growing threats!" Violent students and parents are coming to school and putting educators at risk. Fourteen percent of teachers are victims of physical violence. The administrators fear getting fired and letting unwanted behavior get out of control. Too many inadequate teachers let student behavior get out of control. The quality of teachers is at an all-time low. A few teachers refer to students with "mental crisis!"

It's Not the Student's Fault! Who Should Receive the Blame?

There are many different answers to the question! It all depends on who you ask!

If I were to comment at this point, I would like to see the following happen to our educational system in the U.S.

1.   Eliminate the Federal Department of Education and let each State set its graduation guidelines and rules for operating the school system.

2.   Keep talented teachers and administrators, and get rid of the rest!

3.   Have colleges re-write the admission for becoming a teacher

4.   Have colleges re-write what it takes to become an administrator.

5.   Re-write the behavior rules for students and parents to follow.

6.   Restrict what school laws an attorney can have a part in.

7.   Be able to counter-sue an attorney from school rules.

8.   More pre-school training for teachers and administrators while in college.

9.   6 weeks of training for teachers on handling severe student behavior on an institutional level.

You can agree with me or go your way, but psychology is definitely "NOT" the answer to our educational problem! Like every profession, "you have some bad with the good!" And right now, the BAD has the upper hand!

Another ongoing debate is the "C.C.S.S." Common Core State Standards. Do we want the federal government making lesson plans for K through 12 teachers to follow? "With all the rumors floating around, it's hard to sort out fact from fiction!" This debate has been around for a while. In 2013, the public was left out of the debate.

It's challenging to figure out facts from fiction with all the propaganda swirling around the U.S. I was one of those teachers who lived in the trenches for thirty-eight years. I do "NOT" believe everything a federal office may pass off to the public as fact or even the facts thrown our way that they say are best for our country!

Can our country's educational turmoil be repaired without the input of Federal Department of Education members? "THERE IS WHERE THE MONEY IS GOING," along with a touch of socialistic input from big corporations that enjoy federal money.

We need better guidance and screening of college students who want to go into an educational field, and this is only going to come when the

Colleges can see how easy it is for a person to become a teacher! An old expression from years ago: "Those who can, DO! Those who can't TEACH!

If the money used for developing the new Special Education Departments is no longer going to special education, then where is the money now going? Money is now part of the turmoil in the educational system! The money is now invested into regular classes, and over time, we have taken special needs students and placed them into regular classes, which we call INCLUSION.

That was a very sly and quiet move by the state and federal governments. I can't entirely agree with the thinking of the few who were paid to make that decision. But what can we say to those who say this is best for our educational system? If we disagree with the state board and a few others, they will replace administrators who disagree, or maybe their district will have less money than others! Think About It!

Where have all the good teachers gone? As I said before, they quit! WHY? Many could not handle the stress of teaching for ten years and quit to find a better-paying job.

Suppose the universities and colleges understood that part of the problems and turmoil we have today in the U.S.A. is partially the fault of many fine educational facilities. In that case, the schools of higher learning, such as a college or university, are not making the course as difficult as becoming a teacher and making it as difficult as becoming an attorney in a major university. But they don't, and many teachers don't have the educational background to work and handle students with behavioral problems or attack a teacher or another student! Even in special education, the university would teach different classes or programs for the same subject in special education. Many of the professors have taught the same subject, and it would be taught differently at various colleges by different professors.

I have seen and taught firm, exemplary teachers who had no problems handling students, only to find a weak principal who was afraid of their job and did not support the teacher he needed to help back but was worried.

At the top of this page, I used an old expression, "Those who can—DO! Those who can't ---TEACH! We told the professor who told us that expression, "and those who

"CAN'T TEACH, -- TEACH TEACHERS!" NOW, - Read My Book for a few Pointers You Can Use to Prevent Your Teachers Burnout!

The picture below is a project made by two severe behavior students. They used an overhead projector, cut out Abe Lincoln's picture on black paper, and glued it onto a white poster board. (I still have the poster hanging in my workshop.)

The Plaque below was made in a mold with plaster and mounted on a piece of wood by A student who found another outlet rather than picking on other students. Discipline stopped for him, and he is now a productive citizen in Ohio as a big equipment operator.
Project made by a tenth-grade student in 1976.

Artwork made by Students with Multiple Handicaps and Severe Behavioral Problems. I used "Mainstreaming," which is today referred to as "Inclusion," for those students I tested and ensured they qualified for placement. The projects were sold or taken home as gifts.

CHAPTER 16
Basic Epilepsy Is Common.
Epilepsy is common and is also known as a type of seizure disorder. There are many types of epilepsy. In some people, the cause can be identified. In others, the reason is unknown.

Parts of Epilepsy may be traced to various factors, including:

1.   *Genetic Influence*---Some types may run in families. In these cases, the researchers have linked these to specific genes. Some people have genetic epilepsy that isn't hereditary from a parent.

2.   *Head trauma*—This can be a result of an accident or traumatic injury and can cause epilepsy.

3.   *Factors in the brain*—Brain tumors can cause epilepsy and may also be caused by the way blood vessels form in the brain. People with these malfunctions can have seizures.

4.   *Strokes* over 35 are a leading cause of epilepsy.

5.   *Infections*—Meningitis, HIV, and parasitic infections can be a cause of epilepsy.

6.   *Injury before birth*—Babies are sensitive to brain damage.

7.   *Developmental conditions* — People with epilepsy are most likely to have (ADHD) and other developmental conditions.

Seizures are classified as either Focal or Generalized based on where and how the brain activity causing them begins.

Focal seizures without loss of consciousness, once called simple seizures, may result in body jerking and a loss of awareness. They may also cause a change in body senses such as smell and other similar conditions.

Focal seizures with impaired awareness. Once called complex partial seizures. These involve a loss or change in consciousness. (Like being in a dream).

Sometimes, people with epilepsy may have a behavior change. Symptoms are usually similar from episode to episode.

Over the years, treatments have changed, including medication and sometimes surgery. Some people require lifelong treatment. The cause may be identified for some people, but the reason is unknown for others.

Focal epilepsy is one part of the brain area, and generalized is all the brain. Many different types of seizures occur in other parts of the brain.

What is the difference between Convulsions, seizures, and epilepsy?

1. Convulsion involves uncontrolled, jerky muscle movements and altered consciousness. Some people use the word to refer to a tonic-clonic seizure.

2. Seizures result from abnormal electrical activity in brain cells. You can have a seizure without any symptoms. Seizures are symptoms of epilepsy, but not all seizures are caused by epilepsy.

3. Epilepsy is a neurological disease defined by having multiple, ongoing seizures. Epilepsy can be a life-long condition and has many types listed depending on which part of the brain is affected.

The above information was partly from the "A Guide for Teachers Epilepsy." A teacher's handbook from Alberta, Canada Epilepsy Association 2018.

Case One: Carl Boggs

When Carl first moved to Crestline, Ohio, his records indicated that Carl was diagnosed with what they called in 1969 as "Locomotors System Epilepsy." He had an Aura, gave me a signal, then stood up and started walking. Read the rest of Carl's story below.

During the 1969-1970 school year, Carl was one of my first seventh-grade students who had moved into Crestline, Ohio. After reading Carl's records and testing Carl, I found that Carl had multiple disabilities.

When Carl was younger, he played on a Little League team before players needed to wear helmets. Carl was waiting to bat and was on the sideline warm-up area when the batter swung at the ball, and the bat slipped out of his hand, hitting Carl with the big end of the bat in the temporal lobe area of the brain at full force! Carl was in the Dayton, Ohio, Children's Hospital in a deep coma. Carl's multiple disabilities were a result of the extreme blow to the head.

The terminology for Epilepsy and Seizures was different in the 1960s and 1970s. During that generation, the doctor indicated that Carl had a "Locomotors System Epileptic Seizures." He also had Dyslexia and Dysgraphia, which is the inability to read or write at his age level.

The type of seizures that Carl had was different from other types of Epilepsy. During that time, the two most common forms of epilepsy were what was called "Grand Mal Seizures and Petite Mal Seizures. Over the years, with the new research on seizures, the terminology has changed, and the treatment with medicine and surgery has changed tremendously.

Carl did experience the "Aura," which goes along with some forms of epilepsy. In other words, he could feel the seizure coming on. When he had this feeling, he and I worked out a signal that he was to give me when he thought he was having a seizure.

He just put his hand up into the air and brought his hand back to his side and had the start of his type of seizure. With Carl's type of seizure, it was the same way of starting every time he had his seizure. After the Aura, Carl would stand up and walk, almost like a sleep-walk. I would send another student who was a friend of Carl along with him to ensure he was safe. He would be gone from three to fifteen minutes. When Carl emerged from the seizure, he would grab his head, look around with a half-smile, and return to class. I had made all the other teachers and principals aware of Carl's condition, and the other teachers also knew what to do with Carl if I was not around.

Carl was a super young student from the seventh grade through twelfth grade. He was very athletic in the eighth grade and found a trick he could do with a broom handle that he would unscrew from the broom in our supply room. He would look at me and say, "OK, Coach, let's see you do this!" Carl would grab the broom handle with both hands at about shoulder width, jump over the handle from back to front with both feeds and then jump backward from back to front. And land on his feet without letting go of the broom handle. Any of his classmates that were around would be laughing with Carl. He would look at me and say, "OK, Mr. Stewart, your next!" I would laugh and tell Carl that was an excellent athletic move, and no, I don't want to try your trick with the stick. I'll call you the winner with the tricky stick today. When Carl became a ninth grader, he ran the hurdles in Track for me. Carl would put the handle back in the broom, and everything returned to normal. Only about four of the boys wanted to try the broom trick, so carefully, with a spotter on each side, I let them try. No one could do it, so that was the end of the stick for that year.

From that day on, Carl was my bodyguard. He looked to me as a father figure he never had, and many of the other students in my class didn't as well. They would place an innocent arm on my shoulder or rub my head, which was starting to get a little thin on the back of my head.

The girls and the boys liked me for my fairness (I Think). But they knew if they got a mark on the chalkboard by breaking one of the rules, on Friday, I would give them a quiz, and if they had a mark on the chalkboard, I would take it off if they received a "C" on the quiz.

Carl ran the hurdles on my track team when he became a freshman. He always ended up in third or fourth place and never has a first place. But Carl was well-liked by the other runners because he always told each person, "Good Race!"

Carl struggled with reading and spelling in the seventh and eighth grades but maintained a "C" average. As Carl grew, and by the time he was in the tenth grade, his math was up to a seventh to eighth-grade level, and his reading and spelling were also about the same level.

Carl was well-liked and never used his Epilepsy as an excuse for his grades or any other reason. The Seizures he had during track only affected him a few times while on the team. I restricted his running and the events he would be running in. Carl learned to write in cursive by the time he was in the eleventh grade.

Carl was always helpful with other students in my class and had his school work finished, as well as the work on his projects and helping other students with their projects. He was a handsome young man who worked part-time for a small grocery store as a carry-out. There was a girl in class that Carl liked, and when Carl would have one of his seizures, she would sometimes walk with him and make sure he made it back to class. Carl's seizures would sometimes take him out of the school, but not too far, and we were in the country, so I didn't worry if someone was with him.

When Carl was a senior, he had a job, money in the bank, a girlfriend, Cathy, friends from both students and staff, and could read, write in cursive, and do math on an eighth-grade to beginning ninth-grade level. He was still having his locomotor seizures up to the end of school. On the next to the last day of school, about eleven o'clock in the morning,

Carl gave me his Aura sign, and I told his friend Bill to accompany him. I started to worry when about one-half hour went by, and Carl and Bill were Mrs. Cathy Poffenbaugh Boggs.

Not back to class

Cathy Poffenbaugh
(Boggs)

R.I.P.
Carl Boggs
Class of 1975

In about 50 minutes, Carl and Bill walked into class carrying a box and drinking a milkshake! In the Box. Carl and Bill smiled and said, "Coach, I wanted to give you a treat before I graduated." He then handed me and everyone in the room a small milkshake.

I was when they were not back within ten minutes. Over six years with Carl, I had learned to trust him, and he showed signs of growing into a responsible young adult. When Carl entered the room, I only felt relief! When I saw what he had done as a way to say, "Thank you, Mr. Stewart, for all you have done for us!" I had tears, and then we all drank the milkshakes and laughed. I hugged Carl & Bill, then seven students in the room. We all got up, and we had a "group hug!" I had Carl from grades seven through grade twelve. There was no special education in high school when I started teaching special education. So, six years went fast for Carl, and I must admit that "his milk-shake trick out-did his stick trick!" I never remembered that the "Dairy Delight" he visited was only three blocks away! I still smile about that little trick he pulled! LOL!

Carl graduated in the class of 1975. He got a job and married Cathy Poffenbaugh. Cathy and Carl had children, and in his late twenties, in 1986, Carl died from a Brain Aneurysm from his injury as a child.

Case Two: *David Clever*

"Cerebral Pawsey and Petit Mal Epileptic Seizures"

David was one of my six-year students who started in the 1969-1970 school year. David was a multiple handicap student beginning his seventh-grade year. David had Cerebral Pawsey along with a form of what we use to call Petit Mal epileptic seizures. Having Special Education when it was brand new to the school system was a new beginning and an experience I was looking forward to.

I gave David a signal to provide me with when he felt like he was going into a seizure. He could only use his right arm, so he held it up and made a fist. When Dave went into a seizure, he would shake his head from left to right and move his upper body with ridged motions, then lie his head down on his desk. The whole seizure movement lasted less than four minutes, and as he got older, by the time he was a junior in High School, the seizures were less during the day and lasted less than two minutes per episode.

David's eyes would be closed, and when he awoke, he would look at me, shake his head, and sometimes say something like, "Ah Shit!" And everyone would laugh. I would check if he were all right, then smile at him and tell him jokingly that swearing cost him five points on the board. He would smile back and say only if we can play for a win at chess!

I taught all the students to play chess in the seventh and eighth grades of middle school.

By the time David was out of middle school and into the ninth grade in High School, he had become a fairly good player in chess and would like to challenge me to a game. So would the other students. In the early years of teaching Special Education, I had a paddle hanging in my room. And it rarely saw any use unless I was challenged to chess. If I accepted the challenge, the game between the student and myself would be the loser receiving one swat with the paddle. I never lost and told the student who did lose that if you could show me a "C" on Friday's spelling quiz, I would forget the swat with the paddle. Most students accepted the deal. Most of the time, I would pretend to swing the paddle, tap them, and say, "Keep learning how to play!"

David was also a kitchen helper. He would leave for lunch early enough to eat and help the cooks serve lunch. David was well-liked by everyone who worked in the kitchen. David smiled at all the students coming through the lunch line and talking with many of the ones he knew.

David knew his limitations. If he had an Aura that he was having a seizure, he would give a sign to one of the cooks. They would take Dave around the corner of the kitchen storage area, where he was out of sight, and set him down. David would be back in line serving in a couple of minutes. Everyone knew David had a problem, and everyone was willing to help him when needed.

I had David in school for six years, and his mother and sister ensured his work was complete. David's dad died when he was in School, and they made good helpers for Dave when he needed them the most.

David worked on his art projects; if he needed help, another student was always there to help him finish his project. David did the same for everyone else who asked him for help.

After having David for six years in school, I knew I could trust him when he said his work was completed. He knew how to do all the different forms of math. His language was better, and his reading, spelling, and comprehension were at least on an eighth- or ninth-grade level.

The end of school was drawing near, and David would be graduating this year. As he got older, he became less quiet and louder, saying playful things to me to get my attention. One day, within a couple of weeks of the school year ending, out of nowhere, David's loud voice let out, "HEY, DUDE, Mr. Stewart!" I'm a senior and want to challenge you to a final chess game! I said, "OK, Mr. Clever, you're on, and we'll play two games!" The class laughed and cleared a table for us in the middle of the classroom. They were cheering David on and giving me instructions at the same time.

I told David, "You know what we are playing for with two chess games?" David nodded yes, looked at me, and said, "Be Prepared!" Everyone laughed. The class stood around us like long-lost friends, arms on each other's shoulders. I won the first game and saw a group of special education students coming of age and alive for the first time! David looked at me in the second game and said, "OK, Mr. T! Here I come! I'm all warmed up now!"

I looked around, and everyone was standing around us in a circle. I felt the warmth of the class entering my heart. Not every teacher experiences that feeling, but I did! And that was the type of teacher I wanted to be.

Into the second game, I saw David was making a trap play, so I let him make the play, and he took my queen! The class went nuts and was yelling for David to win. David was working hard, stomping his excellent foot, smiling, chewing his gum, and grinning from ear to ear. He made a few more good moves, which I didn't counter like I would have if I had played an adult or another regular student elsewhere. David moved, looked up from the chess board, smiling from ear to ear at me, and said, "CHECKMATE!"

David's classmates were rubbing his hair and patting his back, and they wanted to put him on their shoulders and parade him in the hall. David had never had so much attention.

The bell rang, and a few students had to go to different classes I had placed them in, such as Music, Beginning Math, Typing, and Shop.

The topic of the swats came up, and David, with a half-grin, said, "Well, what do you say?" I told David that he had to go first, and he didn't want to do that, and I told him that he was going first, and that was how it would be! He agreed.

David walked over to the wall where the hanging paddle had been for years. David looked at me, smiled, and said, "Coach, put your hands on the top of the desk, please. I complied with his command, and suddenly, the class got very quiet again. David moved his arm as far back as he could reach, brought his arm around as fast as he could, and stopped then gave me a gentle tap with the board and said to me, "Mr. Stewart, I can't do it; you've been too good to us, and for me, that's been six years." I said OK, David, it's my turn now. Put your hands on top of the desk. When he did, it got hushed in class again. I started with the paddle, rubbed his rear end with the board, took it back fast, brought it up quickly, and stopped and said to David. "You ready, David?" He was shaking his head yes but had his eyes closed. I took the paddle back and tapped another desk that was in the back of me. I dropped the paddle to the floor, and David turned around, and we hugged each other. David put his arm out, and the kids joined Dave and me in a big group hug. The entire class joined in the group hug, and some had little tears in their eyes. Mainly the seniors! The entire class began laughing and joking until the bell rang at the end of the day. A couple of my friend's teachers asked me what the hell all the noise was happening in your room. I just told everyone we were "Bonding!"

DAVID CLEVER

R.I.P. DAVEY

May the angels sing you to your rest
DIED Wednesday, Feb. 4, 2018
Died at the age of 61. Crestline, Ohio
Loved Ohio State and the Cleveland Browns.

"Treasure and Secretary for Kiwanis Club."

Good night, Sweet Prince. May the Angels Sing You to Your Rest! Coach.
Class of 1975

Chapter 17
Letters of Commendation And Council of Exceptional Children Convention Cleveland, Ohio

I.E.P. Work 1976. I did this with each. Student since 1970! I got the idea from Xavier University. "Where did the Federal Government, I.D.E.A., get THEIR idea from?" I always felt someone stole my thunder!" LOL! Coach!

Bicentennial Year 1976 State of Ohio

CHS teacher Tom Stewart is recognized

Thomas Stewart, of Crestline high school has been selected as the Special Education Teacher of the month for Crawford and Wyandot County.

Mr. Stewart graduated from Ashland College with his B.S. in Physical Education and Biological Sciences. He received his Masters Degree from Xavier University with a Degree in Educating the Emotionally Disturbed. He has completed 12 hours of doctoral work at Bowling Green State University from the Special Education Department.

This year with 18 students in his class, Mr. Stewart has individualized his program completely. He developed his own system. By assessing his students, prescribing their needs, and charting their progress, he can track his students at all times.

Mr. Stewart

Regional Special Education Teacher of the Month

Patty and I are setting up her I.E.P.

I.E.P. Work 1976. I did this with each. Student since 1970! I got the idea from Xavier University. "I wonder where the Federal Government, I.D.E.A., GOT THEIR idea from." I always felt someone stole my thunder!" LOL! Coach!

TEACHER OF THE MONTH BY:

Joan Bauer November 1978

This is the cover of the program that my students handed out to all the people who attended our presentation. The students took my wording and put this program together. (Coach).

OHIO FEDERATION
COUNCIL FOR EXCEPTIONAL CHILDREN

Marching To The Tune Of A Different Drummer

by:
CRESTLINE WORK-STUDY CLASS
Crestline High School
Oldfield Rd.
Crestline, Ohio
44827

Instructor: Telephone:
Thomas J. Stewart, B.S., M.S.   1-419-683-1964

"If a man does not keep
pace with his companions,
perhaps it is because he
hears a different drummer.
Let him step to the music
which he hears."
by Henry David Thoreau

Thomas Stewart, Work-Study Program Teacher from Crestline, Ohio.

Joan Bauer took over as The North Central District Coordinator of Special Education from Joe Morman's office in 1978.

Walking down the upstairs corridor at Crestline High School, you will notice that the activity center is Tom's class; it is upstairs, and everyone can see it! Please don't call it an E.M.R. Class or Special Education. Tom has built up the prestige of his class by insisting this is a "Work-Study Class," and he will defend his students if someone thinks otherwise. The success of his program has a lot to do with public relations, projects, and success in the classroom and the field of work.

First, a little background on Tom. He graduated from Ashland College with a Bachelor of Science in Biological Science and Physical Education. He received his Master's in educating the emotionally disturbed from Xavier University in Cincinnati, Ohio. Tom has been working on his Dissertation for his Ph.D. in Special Education.

In 1976, Mr. Stewart and his class were asked to give a presentation to the State of Ohio's Council of Exceptional Children at the Bond Court Hotel in downtown Cleveland, Ohio.

Mr. Stewart and his class developed a program that individualizes classroom instructions and uses student art to "Motivate the Reluctant Learner!" Four of Tom's classroom students presented "Individualizing Educational Instructions" and "Using Art as a Means of Motivation for Severe Behavior Disorder Children."

This year, with eighteen students in his class, Tom has wholly individualized his class and developed his system of assessing students, prescribing their needs, and charting their progress. As a result, he can track his students' progress in every subject.

Academically, he enjoys working the arts and crafts with his students. The class sells the products they make, and each student takes turns counting the money and decides how it will be spent. At the top of the list was a stereo for the classroom. Part of the money is put into the class treasury for events such as field trips.

The class has taken Field Trips to the Cleveland Art Museum and Wright-Patterson Air Force Base Museum in Dayton, Ohio, Mohican State Park in Loudonville, Ohio, and riding a Riverboat at Rosco Village in Coshocton, Ohio.

Take some time to visit Tom's classroom; it will be worth the visit.

Written by: Joan Bauer

1976 was the Bicentennial Year, and we were asked to show the State of Ohio teachers, administrators, and state education officials what individual students could do if they completed their lessons. Most students have two or three classes they are "Mainstreamed" into. If we were discussing the present education, we would use "Inclusion."

Getting the class ready for the Convention was not easy. I spent most of my spare time writing what I felt was essential to present, and the students used their time making reports to accompany their classroom projects.

The following is the *"Heart of my Book!"* It is also a part of my Heart and Soul of how I feel about education! It should be a part of all Teachers' and Parents' goals to help their students or their Children. I CALL IT:

Classroom Climate Control:

"This was the central part of our presentation at the State C.E.C. Convention."

The Heart of our Presentation

Classroom Climate Control:

Plan your activities carefully. (This helps reduce disorder.)

A.   Select your material realistically.

B.   Know and use your student's interests and experience.

C.   Promote self-direction (Let the student help you plan.)

D.   Be specific, consistent, and straightforward in your rules.

E.   Put the ACCENT on the POSITIVE rather than the NEGATIVE.

F.   Try to stress accomplishment and encouragement. (Success motivates, and Praise attracts.)

G.   Provide an opportunity for free choice.

H.   Don't talk too much. (You don't have to master-mind everything.)

I.   Save your threats. (You usually regret making them anyway.)

J.   NO Debates! (Once you make a decision or judgment, make it Final!)

**Written for the Ohio State Council of Exceptional Children,
1976 Bicentennial Convention
In Cleveland, Ohio
By:
Thomas Stewart. B.S/M.S.**

Emphasis on Social Aspects of Teaching Are:

A.   Student Emotional Control.

B.   Co-operation.

C.   Responsibility.

D.   Self-Respect.

E.   Individual Pride.

F.   TEACHER – Student Personal Relationship.

G.   De-Emphasizing Competition for Grades.

If all teachers show the social aspects written for them by many great people, what more does a teacher want? It does not matter if your class is a regular class with multiple disabled students, such as an Inclusion class, or a Special Education class with only students who have numerous problems, such as Severe Behavior Disorder! IT'S THE TEACHER STANDING IN FRONT OF THE CLASS! Or The PARENT, making the right decision for their child!

QUITTING HAS NEVER ENTERED MY MIND! NEVER!!

I said it before, and I'll repeat it! Universities and Colleges make their Education Departments "TOO DAMN EASY TO APPLY FOR!!!" The students taught by the higher learning Colleges and Universities should require more "Behavioral on-the-job training" in grades one through six-or, seven through twelve!

"Students Need Hands-On Experience!"

Form I had to fill out for the C.E.C. 1796 Bicentennial Convention.

ANNUAL CONVENTION
1976

OHIO FEDERATION
COUNCIL FOR EXCEPTIONAL CHILDREN

SESSION DETAIL FORM

(To be completed by Session Presenter)

NOTE: Session Presenters are asked to give this information for th
essions for which they have agreed to present and return this form t
r. Anne K. Petry, Director, Office of Special Education, Akron Publi
chools, 65 Steiner Avenue, Akron, Ohio 44301, by May 24, 1976. The
ession detail for the convention program will be taken directly fro
his form. Please be advised that there are electrical outlets in e
f the rooms being utilized for meetings; however, it is the respons
ility of the session presenters to see that any equipment (projecto
ecorders, screens, extension cords, etc.), which may be needed, is
vailable.

SESSION: B. C. H
10:30 - 12   (Number to be assigned)   ALFRED
                          N. 12
8:30 - 10:15 a.m.   DATE: Nov. 13, 1976   ROOM: Sammy Kaye
(To be assigned)   (To be as

F PRESENTATION: The Use of Arts & Craft to Motivate Ac

OF PRESENTATION: " FUN, PROFIT, LEARNING" For The H.S.

          Work-Study Class. or "See More, Do
                                    More".

T: (Slide Presentation) The place of individualized
   in the classroom. Using a main theme as a class
   Using Arts and Crafts to stimulate interest and
   main theme. Also, how to earn money for the non
   The main part of the presentation, is geared f
   of Special Education but specifically E.M.R.

PRESENTER: Mr. Thomas Stewart

Title: E.M.R. Work-Study Instr.

ploying Agency: Crestline H.S. Crestline, Oh.

siness Address: Crestline HS Oldfield Rd. Crestl

AMEN

Northcentral Ohio
Special Education Service Center

TITLE VI-B, EHA

791 Williamsburg Dr.
Galion, Ohio 44833
Phone (419) 468-6447

November 17, 1976

DIRECTOR
R. Paul McMillan

IRC COORDINATOR
Joseph T. Morman

CONSULTANT
SPEECH THERAPY
Sherod Guzay

Mr. Thomas Stewart
Crestline High School
Oldfield Rd. Rt. #2
Crestline, OH 44827

Dear Tom,

Paul and I want to commend you on the fine job
you did at the CEC Conference. Congratulations
are certainly also due to the members of your class
who made those inspiring presentations. They certainly are a credit to your school.

Enclosed is my check to pay for the eagle placque
you let me take on credit. I will display it in
my office as an example of the fine work your students
do.

Our region is proud of your Work-Study Program.
It serves as a fine example of what can be done
if the teacher is willing to put his heart and soul
into his work.

Sincerely,

Joseph T. Morman

Joseph T. Morman
IRC Coordinator

encl.
cc. Charles Brown, Superintendent
Stephen Mabee, Principal

JTM/pas

Letter Of Commendation from State Regional Office to: Thomas Stewart -Author.

Northcentral Ohio
Special Education Service Center
TITLE VI-B, BHA

701 Wittenberg Dr.
Galion, Ohio 44833
Phone (419) 468-0447

October 6, 1976

DIRECTOR
R. Paul McMillen

IRC COORDINATOR
Joseph T. Norman

CONSULTANT
SPEECH THERAPY
Sherrel Clump

FISCAL AGENT:

Crawford County
Board of Education

PARTICIPATING SCHOOLS:

ASHLAND COUNTY

Ashland City
Hillsdale Local
Loudonville Perrysville EV
Mapleton Local

CRAWFORD COUNTY

Buckeye Central Local
Bucyrus City
Colonel Crawford Local
Crestline EV
Galion City
Wynford Local

KNOX COUNTY

Centerburg Local
Danville Local
East Knox Local
Fredericktown Local
Mt. Vernon City

MARION COUNTY

Elgin Local
Marion City
Pleasant Local
Ridgedale Local
River Valley Local

MORROW COUNTY

Cardington-Lincoln Local
Highland Local
Mt. Gilead EV
Northmor Local

RICHLAND COUNTY

Clear Fork Valley Local
Crestview Local
Lexington Local
Lucas Local
Madison Local
Mansfield City
Ontario Local
Plymouth Local
Shelby City

WYANDOT COUNTY

Carey EV
Mohawk Local
Upper Sandusky EV

Mr. Charles Brown, Supt.
Crestline School Admin. Bldg.
S. Thoman St.
Crestline, OH 44827

Dear Mr. Brown;

I'm sure you were pleased to hear that the Crestline High School Work Study Class was selected as an excellent class model and asked to make a presentation at the State CEC Convention in Cleveland, Ohio on November 12 and 13.

We're proud too, that your Mr. Tom Stewart was recognized for his fine work in this area. We would like other Work Study teachers of our region to have the chance to get to know Tom and see some of his ideas in action at the CEC Convention.

As per my conversation with you on Friday, October 1, we at the Special Education Service Center will be glad to help Tom in terms of finances he needs to take his project and the four students who will be making the presentation to Cleveland.

If you can furnish Tom with the finances he needs now, to make this trip, we will contract with you to use Tom's services as a consultant next Spring (1977) and pay you the amount of Tom's actual expenses, not to exceed $250.00.

I have discussed this plan with Tom and he has agreed, provided it meets with your approval.

Hoping to hear from you soon, I am.

Sincerely,

Joseph T. Norman

Joseph T. Norman
IRC Coordinator

P.S. This agreement will have the approval by the Crawford County Bd. of Educ. at this meeting on Oct 18.
JTN

cc. Tomas Stewart
JTN/pas

Letter of Commendation to Superintendent from State of Ohio Regional Office.

MANSFIELD PUBLIC SCHOOLS
MANSFIELD, OHIO

Pupil Services Center
270 West Sixth Street
Mansfield, Ohio 44902
May 12, 1977

Mr. Thomas J. Stewart
Crestline High School
Oldfield Road
Crestline, Ohio 44827

Dear Mr. Stewart:

I want to thank you and the pupils in the Work-Study Class for the excellent presentation of the activities which occur in your classroom.

Teachers such as yourself are the ones who make special education really "special" to those who need it most. The pupils' outstanding behavior reflects your concern for them.

The film presentation made it clear that the students are motivated and do try to do their best.

Thanks again to you and your students.

Sincerely,

Nancy L. McConnell

Mrs. Nancy L. McConnell
Coordinator
Practical Learning Program

cjc

The above letter was sent to me as a "Thank You" for coming to Mansfield Public Schools with four students and presenting our class's audio-video slide Presentation. We also gave presentations to other schools in our part of Ohio.

105

Crestline High School

Phone 683 2964

Frank Coughlin, Principal
Nick Konya, Counselor

7654 Crestland Rd.
Crestline, Ohio 44827

March 29, 1990

Mr. John Edgar, Superintendent
Crestline Exempted Village School District
Crestline, Ohio 44827

Re: Narrative Summary for Mr. Tom Stewart

Dear Mr. Edgar:

This narrative summary is written in comply with the Crestline Certificated Staff Appraisal Model.

Mr. Tom Stewart has been employed by the Crestline Exempted Village School district for twenty-one years and has been teaching for a total of twenty-five years.

Mr. Tom Stewart teaches the Developmentally Handicapped class and was observed teaching periods 2, 3, 4, and 5 on October 18, 1989, November 29, 1989, January 23, 1990 and February 27, 1990.

Strengths

Mr. Stewart runs a fine program. He is deeply involved with his students and keenly aware of their individual needs. He gives them many opportunities to improve themselves, both personally and scholastically. Tom seems to have a good grasp of what the students want to accomplish and is able to develop units that directly reinforce their goals. The additional help with Christmas presents, job interviews, art projects, etc., speaks well to your commitment to the kids.

Suggestions

Let's continue to plan together on the work study program. It has paid big dividends for Rudel this year. I think it can serve as a large motivating factor for the young students.

Sincerely,

Frank Coughlin
Principal

(Mr.) Tom Stewart

Mr. Frank Coughlin

133

106

We did multiple school presentations in our area of Ohio.

Every picture in this book is from the Film Slide presentation. The cassette contained approximately 60 slides, and each student had a two—or more-minute-long vocal conversation about what they did in class.

My manners class was instrumental for the four boys I took with me. Many adults in attendance were delighted with our class presentation and engaged in conversations with the boys and me. The boys were also successful in selling class-made projects and were praised by the teachers, administrators, and state officials from different states who were attending. The boys used "Yes, No, Yes-Sir" and polite gestures such as "Thank You." I was proud of the four students; each had their personality! All four were seniors and eighteen years old. They had a name tag on them, and I was not afraid of them answering questions improperly. They had spent money given to us by the regional office and made close to one thousand dollars in the sales of their projects. This success in sales is a testament to their hard work and dedication. One student's name is Terry, and Terry has a personality that sometimes takes a little getting used to. He liked to imitate people. He would use the secretary's voice from the office, sneak into the back room, and, using the secretary's voice, get on the intercom and say, "Mr. DiPietro, line one," then sneak out of the office. Everyone swore it was Betty. But I knew better after a while. I just told Terry, NO MORE! And it stopped. Thursday evening, after our first presentation, I couldn't find Terry. He was a good-looking, tall student dressed in a sports coat who looked older than eighteen. I walked upstairs one floor to an open room they had set up for the Adults in attendance for a wine-tasting room sponsored by a couple of businesses in the Cleveland, Ohio area.

I looked around the large area, and I found my tall, good-looking student talking to two ladies who were wearing nametags with their school's name on the tag. The ladies were holding a glass of wine, and Terry was holding an empty glass with his "Nametag" on the lapel of his jacket. I walked up to Terry, tapped him on the shoulder, and said, Hello, Mr. Miller. May I have a word with you for a moment? Terry's face turned different shades of red, and I didn't want to embarrass him in front of the two ladies. We walked toward the hallway, and I told Terry very quietly, "Get your ass back down to the room!"

He apologized and said, "He didn't have any wine to drink, but he got a young teacher's phone number and smiled!" The other guys laughed, and then I just shook my head and said nothing more. I told the four young guys that I trusted them to be back in the room by ten. We have another program in the morning.

(I was told she did call him! That's what I was told! A-h-h-h, To Be 18 Again!) LOL!

STUDENT ART FOR CONVENTION

This is the downtown Bond Court Hotel and our State C.E.C. Cover for the 1976 Bicentennial Convention.

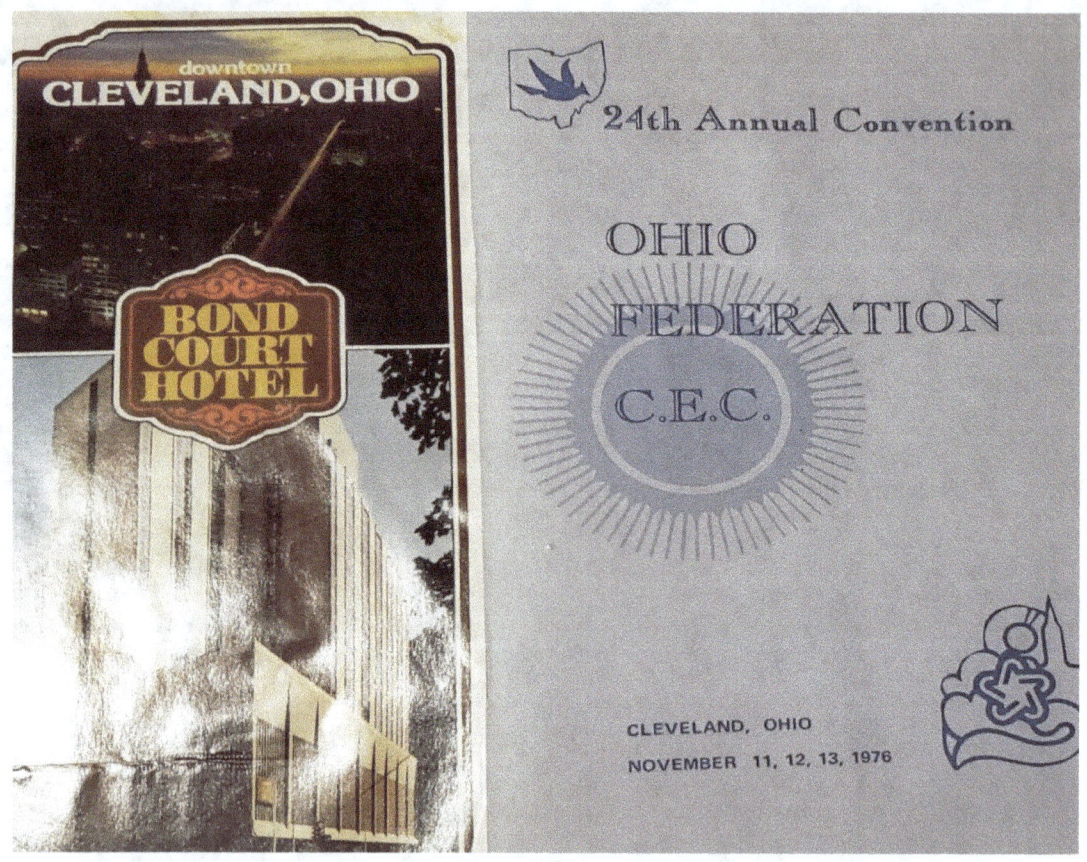

It was time for us to be called onto the stage in front of a large crowd of professional people.

We had everything ready to go, and I had just remembered who I had with me that day, where they were three and four years ago, what they were then, and what they represented now. We were all a little nervous except for Terry. He was having a ball, talking, and waving to people in the front row. He was using, *Yes Sir and Yes Ma'am.*

At school, Terry could imitate one of the secretaries from the office over the intercom system, and the teacher would come to the office thinking they were called down. (There were no cell phones during this generation.) This was one of his little pranks during lunchtime. I found out who was doing it and told him, "No More!" It was funny, and I could have made his life miserable, but when I said stop, he would listen to me and just smile at me.

From experience, I knew that looking at the audience in the eyes would make you more nervous. So, I told the guys to focus their eyes above the people's heads.

We had everything set up on the stage: tables, Student Projects, and a slide projector with sound. We were introduced, and three of the boys were in place when we were introduced, but Jerry was walking toward me with a smile. He had been in the front of the stage talking with people in the front row. Without thinking, I took the Microphone held up to Terry and said, "Wow, Terry! Look at all the People! Wonder what John Wayne would say?" Without blinking, Terry looked around, stuck his thumbs in his belt, and then spoke like John Wayne and said, "Well, I'll Tell-Ya Pilgrim, I think we better get on our white horses and get the hell out of here!" The crowd went wild with Terry's sense of humor and stage behavior and laughed and clapped more for that moment than any other during the Convention. The "Special Education Presentation" was a big hit! YOU CAN TEACH STUDENTS TO DO ANYTHING YOU WANT IF YOU KNOW WHAT YOU'RE DOING AS A TEACHER! Do Your Homework, Be Prepared, Read My Book for Little Hints, and Get Ready for A New Year!

**At the Presentation's end, people called for Terry to take a BOW! He did!

I was the guest speaker at the Lions Club in the 1969/70 school year. They wanted me to discuss the upcoming Special Education program in our Junior High School system.

OHIO FEDERATION
Council For
Exceptional Children
24th Annual
State Convention

NOVEMBER 11, 12, 13, 1976
BOND COURT HOTEL
Cleveland, Ohio

THURSDAY
November 11, 1976

4:00 pm — 9:00 pm . . . . Registration (Lobby)

Ohio Association Of Special Education Administrators

9:00 am	Registration — Coffee — Rolls
9:30 am	Program Overview
10:00 am	Film Presentation — 94:142 Discussion
11:45 am	Luncheon — $8.00
1:15 pm	Administrative Consideration regarding special education laws, new standards, and implications for schools, parents and children — Panel Presentation
3:15 pm	Ohio Department of Special Education Staff
4:45 pm	Social Hour with I.U.C. — Cash Bar

Inner-University Council For Special Education

10:00 am	Update on Ohio's Higher Education State

This was sent out to all the schools in Ohio and the surrounding states.

111

The title of our program was:
"Marching To the Tune of a Different Drummer."
By: Henry David Thoreau:
"If a man does not keep pace with his companions,
Perhaps it is because he hears a different drummer.
Let him step to the music that he hears!"

I selected this saying by Henry David Thoreau because it addresses every student involved in a Special Education program around our country, regardless of what type it is.

All the pictures in my book were on the cassette we played at the convention, and every student had a speaking part. Each student said what they did regarding schoolwork in the classroom and what they enjoyed the most about being in my room. They all thought I was a fair teacher because each was graded individually and not compared to another student.

When our program ended on Saturday, Teachers and Administrators from around the state approached my students and me and congratulated them on a job well done. One Toledo, Ohio, administrator said, "That was a very good job by a Special Education Class!"

I didn't have a chance to say anything, but one student turned around, looked toward the administrator, and said, "Sir, we refer to our class at Crestline High School as the Work-Study Class." I spoke up and told the person that we had changed the name from E.M.R. Work Study to what it was not in 1973. I thought it sounded better, and the administrators and school board followed the new name. Other administrators, came up to me and asked if we could visit their school and show how to get the type of behavior in a class I showed at the convention. My four students and I went to five school districts in our state area.

On the way home, each person in the van was trying to talk at the same time, and they were laughing at different things that happened to each other. I was tired, and not only that, but I had close to eight hundred dollars in a zipper bag from the projects my students made for the Convention and sold to the people who attended. Our class fund grew into a sizable sum of money for the students.

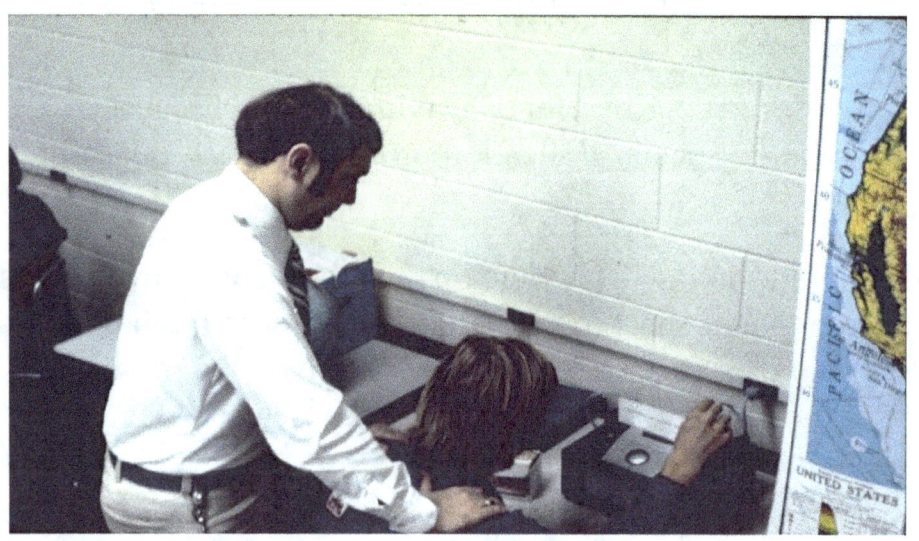

Projects Made By Students for the Convention, the Room, and as Gifts.

The Chess Board was made by one of my students who was dyslexic and had Dysgraphia but was good with his hands. The Chess Pieces were made by another of my students in our back room. At the beginning of his ninth grade, he had a behavior problem. I placed both boys and other students into the school's Shop Class. In time, both students changed into responsible students. The reading and writing for the one became better, and the behavior and attitude of the second student changed. When the students found out that our class was chosen to put on a presentation for the State of Ohio C.E.C. Convention, all wanted to help, but I decided these two students should go with me because they both were upperclassmen, worked hard, and had Ideas that we could and did use. The slide presentation was their idea, along with other brainstorms. They did the photography for the most part, and I chose the two other students I took along because of how much they contributed as well.

Chapter 18
The Work-Study Part Of The Class

We added a new subject to our curriculum. We were referred to as E.M.R. Special Education, but after talking to the Superintendent and the Board of Education, we changed it to E.M.R. Work-Study Education. After a while, I dropped the E.M.R. and referred to my class as the "Work-Study Program." However, on the records, it was still a Class for students with special needs.

The students learned how to apply for jobs and how to handle themselves on a job. A ninth- and tenth-grade student could get out of school during the last period of the day depending on his age, whether his school work was up to date, and whether he had a part-time job to go to. The junior could get out of school at noon if they had a job to go to, and the senior who had all of his graduation requirements completed and only needed English as a fourth-year student would not come to school except for Friday. He would come in on Fridays and show me his bank savings account and updated work on all subjects he would be responsible for. Then, he would go back to his job.

I would use my planning period to travel to Crestline and sometimes neighboring towns to look for jobs for potential students and check on students with their employers to see if everything was going well or if there was anything I could do to help them. Read the past chapter about Greg. He was a worker and worked part-time as a contractor. After graduation, he worked for Diaz Construction. Greg learned to read Boue-Prints and became a general contractor himself. He would hire subcontractors to do plumbing and other, sometimes electrical, work. He was the general contractor for a brick restaurant in Crestline called," Hunger Paynes.

Greg also worked for Mr. King as a contractor. Greg was good in math, and I told the teacher I was placing one of my students into one of her beginning math classes at the beginning of the school year. I told her which one and asked how he was doing so far. When I asked the teacher about Greg and how he was doing, she was surprised to find out he was a student with Dyslexia. She was pleasantly surprised that Greg was the one. This is Richard on the Left and Greg on the Right. This is a musket that was made for the Bicentennial. Richard is also good with their hands, and both received an A grade while enrolled in shop class.

Greg made the Board

Richard made the chess pieces.

Greg also worked for Mr. King as a contractor. Greg was good in math, and I told the teacher I was placing one of my students into one of her beginning math classes at the beginning of the school year. I told her which one and asked how he was doing so far. When I asked the math teacher, Mrs. Alguire, about Greg and how he was doing, she was surprised to find out he was a student with Dyslexia and was doing well. Richard and Greg are also good with their hands, and both received an A grade while enrolled in shop class.

Many of the multi-handicapped students, such as a student with Cerebral Palsy or Epilepsy, were restricted from working in public employment due to the lack of use of a hand, leg, seizure, or transportation. With these students, I was able to find a couple of jobs for them, such as helping to clean individuals' homes, and a few jobs at school, such as the kitchen or Library.

I had industries in neighboring towns that would call me to hire girls of color. They would tell me if the Timpkin Company personnel office was short of female or black employees. This was due to the Federal Contracts they would receive if they had the quota of employees up to date correctly.

After graduation, many of my students had good jobs. One student was hired by General Motors in Mansfield, Ohio. Many students found higher-paying jobs after graduation in Crestline, Ohio factories or other employers such as Krogers and other food chains. One girl spent her life as a Cashier at Krogers in Bucyrus, Ohio. Hospitals and Nursing homes hired a few of my students as well. A few of my graduates returned to technical school to take a couple of classes for the company they are working for. Most students I have had in school over the years are either retired or still working. Many of my students from the early years tell me thank you for teaching us how to apply for a job; it worked!

The shop class. After High School, Richard was hired to help install the giant windmills that generate electrical power. That's not for me. I'll keep my feet on the ground; thank you!!

As a young student, he seemed to eat a lot, but he never put on weight, and he grew to be at least six feet three inches tall. Art was my way of keeping Richard in line. He had a chance to work for a Lithographing Company that made artwork, including Calendars and Church directories. Richard became more pleasant and easier to work with as he grew older. In this book, you will find a picture of Indian Maidens that Richard made out of different-colored sand. Richard was a big help when our class attended the State C.E.C. Convention. Richard put tremendous effort into what we had to do as a class to complete everything for our trip to Cleveland, Ohio. He helped students who needed help and encouraged them just as I would have. He was a great assistant!

Cindy Scheiber and Sandy Carroll, along with many of the other students, have been friends throughout school and are still friends today. Cindy comes from a family where a few family members have albinism, an inherited condition that affects the eyes and hair color, and very light skin due to a lack of melanin in the skin pigment. Today, she watches over her grandchildren.

Sandy Carroll was waiting for the bell to ring. Darryell's sister, Sandy, is working on her history assignment. Sandy has Cerebral Palsy and is very quiet. Sandy had problems with her Reading, Math, Spelling, and Writing. She was a real sweetheart. She always was a student who tried her best at everything she tried. Today, her family is grown up, and she enjoys he grandchildren. She is still as sweet as when she was in High School. Sandy started with me when I began teaching Junior High School. Sandy was the youngest of eight children.

Not all of my students were behavioral or born with multiple problems. A few just lacked the parenting it takes to raise a child from birth until they become a young adult. Many parents try the skills themselves to train or teach their youngsters how to read or write because they do not know how either. I have visited homes where the mother has told me she couldn't help their child because she didn't know herself. It took one mother a lot of guts and a few tears for a parent to admit that to a teacher. That is why I feel it is essential for a teacher to visit a student's home. The mother told me through tears that she couldn't read or write. I asked her, Point-blank, "Would you like to learn?" She told me, "There's nothing I would rather learn in this world! Oh-Yes!" I told her I would see that she got books on her assignments from her daughter and graded her work. Mrs. King attended school with her daughter for part of a day to learn. I had her help me set up a time when she would be in school, and I also set up an "I.E.P" for Reading, Spelling, Writing, and Beginning Math. She learned well, and it was also suitable for the students I had in class to have an adult to talk to.

Throughout the years of teaching High School, I had a few mothers and fathers ask for the same kind of help as Mrs. King. They wanted to help their children like many other parents, but they didn't have the background growing up to have parents with skills to help them.

Most of the school knew I occasionally had a parent or two come to class. The Superintendent I had at the time didn't see anything wrong with having them come to my class. One principal looked at me and smiled when he walked into my room to evaluate my teaching and saw a mother different from Mrs. King. He looked at her and said jokingly, "Mr. Stewart, you know you can't have this young student in here!" The class laughed, and I introduced him to Mrs. Mullins.

Cindy Schieber is studying for her Friday quiz.

Lelia, .and Speed Reading. Lelia had no real problems in school except for her reading, spelling, and writing. Her father was in the Air Force, and they had moved so many times over her education that she was behind. But upon graduation, she was doing fine. Today, I heard from her on Facebook, and she lives out of state.

Lelia Harris is working on a machine called the "Guided Reader." You can control the Degree of difficulty, age group, and the speed of your reading.

Chapter 19
Innovative Ideas for Classroom Teachers
Making Positive Relationships with their students.

(Also Good for Parents to Try!)

In today's modern schools, I'm sure the teacher has everything they need, with computers, programs, and all the other equipment at their disposal! As long as the student has a "Teacher who cares," that's Important! So-o-o, you mean that there are a few educators who don't care or, should I say, give a S _ _ _! (My Opinion! I have heard and read from Teachers, Parents, and a few Administrators telling me how hard it is to find good teachers who are capable of correctly handling today's students properly).

I have been told by teachers who care that many of the teachers they work with feel they should be in another profession because they are having a hard time handling the students' behavior. After reading my book I hope you will find a few ideas that may help you decide if you really want to be a teacher or not. Not every person will feel the same way about education as I did. I wish I could have stayed for another ten or more years. I loved my students and my teaching, as well as the many years of coaching. Art projects can help a reluctant student use more self-control, and I have always made that goal important to the entire class. They must follow the classroom rules if they want to work on their projects. The remainder of the class saw the first completed project and wanted to finish theirs or make one of their own. This IS WHAT I ALWAYS WANTED TO SEE FROM MY CLASS, - - A Positive Attitude and a willingness to try something new.

During the beginning of Junior High Special Education, a few students could not form friendships with other students or their teachers. After testing my students with the "Peabody Individual Achievement Test (P.I.A.T.), I found that many of my students were low in their academic abilities as well as some were considered, (S.B.D.), Severe Behavior Disorders and a few (A.D.D.) Attention Deficit Disorder

Dyscalculia is the inability to do simple math, and Dyslexia and Dysgraphia are the inability to read and write—many of the students with these disabilities. I used part of my Federal Flow through Money that I received to purchase hardware and software that would help develop multisensory and manipulative skills in reading, spelling, comprehension and math that were intended for various levels of learning. We did not have computers or the software for computers during that generation of the 1960's or 1970's.

I set up programs for every student's level of understanding they were comfortable starting with. Over a four- or six-year period, I felt most of the students achieved their goal if they were on a 6th, 7th, or 8th-grade level in reading and math. A few accomplished a little higher than the 10th-grade level. I felt I always gave each student my time and dedicated attention. I would also notice personal things about each of my students.

The first and most important thing I wanted to do with any of my students was to create an environment with less anxiety in the classroom for any of the young students with developmental disabilities.

Below are four random "Fun Puzzles" that the students really enjoyed working on in teams.

Have Fun!

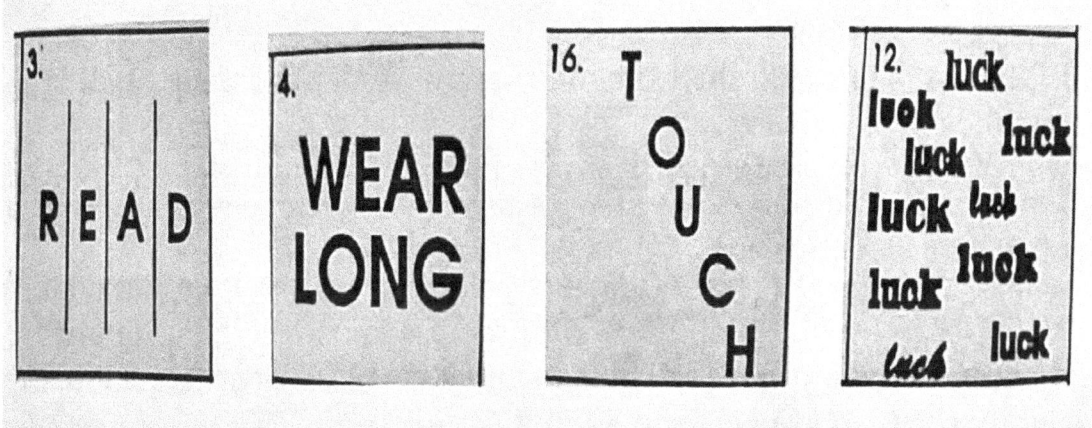

After testing the Junior High Students with the Peabody Test, I knew what each student could do in each subject. Then, I could be creative and divide the class into four teams, doing my best to make the teams even as much as possible, depending on who was there that day or period. I wanted them to know N.S.E.W., Time-of-Day, and Times-tables; the list would also include geography. I would give the list to the four groups, and they would have one or two periods to study with each other, making sure that each person in their group knew the answers.

We would work on the spelling list the same way for a prize, not a grade.

However, each student had a list of spelling words for which they were responsible.

I'll finish this Chapter by giving you ten ways that a teacher can use to create a better relationship between the Teacher the Pupil, or the Student. ** Parents can use these ten ways with their children as well.

RELATIONSHIP OF TEACHERS TO STUDENTS (PUPILS)

For Parents with Children as well

•   Teachers should guide and direct their students but not dominate them. They should be kind and sympathetic but firm.

•   Teachers should give constructive rather than destructive criticism; occasional favorable comments will improve student morale.

•   Teachers should not invite impudence, disrespect, or indignity from students. While teachers should always have a friendly and interested attitude toward the students, they should maintain a certain reserve so that relations do not border on familiarity.

•   Teachers should refrain from discussing students in any place where a student is likely to overhear.

•   Teachers should not give a student a permit when they know that another teacher has denied permission.

•   When carrying out administrative orders against their judgment, teachers should not reveal their attitude to students; they should make the students feel that there is unity between teachers and administration.

•   No teacher should allow criticism of another teacher to be voiced in their classroom, nor should the teacher consent to hearing it from a student.

•   Teachers should not allow a student's social status to influence them in classroom activities.

•   Teachers should settle all misunderstandings with the person directly concerned and go to the principal only when it is impossible to settle otherwise.

•   Teachers should expect no more in the way of courteous treatment than they are willing to accord supervisors, other teachers, their students, and the parents of their students.

ANSWERS TO FUN PUZZLES:

    1. READ BETWEEN THE LINES.

    2. LONG UNDERWEAR.

    3. TOUCH DOWN.

    4. LOTS OF LUCK.

Chapter 20
Some Do's and Don'ts for Teachers Also
Control, Success, Respect & Warmth

For Teachers and Parents

Manner Of Expressing Oneself Has Powerful Effect Upon Students.

The following self-assessment won't, of course, give you all the answers as to what you should or should not do in class - - that's up to you! But it may give you some idea of how successful you are in creating positive self- images in your students and - - perhaps more important – determine if you have a positive attitude toward your students.

Dos for Teachers:
- Do be JUST in requirements and in making realistic assignments of lessons.
- Do strive to be fair in all situations.
- Do show courtesies in relation to students.
- Do consult parents and use tact when doing so. Home visits are best.
- Do be consistent in disciplining.
- Do show trust and Confidence in students.
- Do make efforts to draw out and encourage the shy and submissive student.
- Don't For Teachers:
- Don't talk about the misdeeds of a student except to those who are concerned.
- Don't give school work as a punitive measure.
- Don't criticize the work of another teacher.
- Don't show dislike for any student.
- Don't make derogatory comments towards parents.
- Don't speak or act toward a student in a manner that is undisciplined or unacceptable.

The following is a list of Options within regular and special classrooms or the Inclusion Classroom that may benefit students. Any classroom teacher willing to alter the usual procedure and committed to helping students should find the above (Do's) and (Do not) and the following relatively simple to initiate.

Control
- Do I make sure that I am adequately prepared for class?
- Do I arrive in class before my students?
- Do I teach in as exciting and engaging manner as possible?
- Do I remember to think of minor discipline problems as understandable events?

- Do I give proper assignments: not too easy, not too hard, too vague, or too dull?
- Do I avoid having favorites?
- Do my students have room to be active and natural?
- Do I have a clear idea of what is and is not acceptable in my class?

Success
- Do I ensure that every student has a reasonable chance of success today?
- Do I give my students a chance to be trustworthy?
- Do I delegate responsibility to students?
- Do I take special opportunities to praise students for their successes?
- Do I make generally positive comments on written work?
- Do I give extra support and encouragement to slow-working students?
- Do I give tasks which are, and which appear to the student to be, within their abilities?
- Do I allow my students to make mistakes without penalty?
- Do I recognize the success of students for what they did earlier?

Respect
- Do I permit students to challenge my opinion? If money is needed for a show, activity, or project, do I let the students earn the money in class when possible?
- Do I allow the students to help formulate the rules they are asked to follow?
- Do I give the students a voice in planning?
- Do I learn the name of each student as soon as possible?
- Do I show special interest in any observations students make or problems they may have?
- Do I talk with students, not just at them?
- Do I encourage students to try something new and to join new activities?
- Do I encourage each student to make contributions to the class, and am I generous in my reactions?

Warmth
- Do I share my feelings with my students? (Laughter, anger, excitement, etc.)
- Do I welcome every student individually at the beginning of class if I have a chance?
- Do I say goodbye to as many students as possible at the close of class?
- Do I notice and comment favorably on the things that are important to students?
- Do I spread my attention around and include each student?
- Do I keep a special watch for the student who may need special attention?

Why science teachers
should not be given
playground duty.

Below is a letter I received from my 1972 graduating class. The graduates composed the letter and gave it to me the Friday before graduation. The way it was written brought tears to my eyes. All six graduates had a part in writing this letter 52 years ago!

To Mr. Stewart,
from the Senior class
of "72".

Dear Mr. Stewart:

You are a real great guy. If all of us Seniors had to do all over in school we would still like to have you for our teacher because we know as well as all the Seniors in this class has learned a lot. We are writing this letter to you because we all want to thank you so very much for all you have done for us Seniors but we just don't know how to tell you thanks. But anyhow all of us Seniors in this class would like to tell you thanks for everything that you have done for all of us Seniors in this class. But anywhere you go and everything you do don't forget the class of "72" because we all will not forget you because we all like you so very much as a nice teacher. Where ever you go think about us alot because we all will think about you everywhere we go and how good you were to all of us Seniors. And about all the ways you helped us in any way you could and he will help all the other kids in every way he can to get through C.H.S. And I know that some of us lied to you but you keep right on helping us, and I know he got so mad at us that could of beat the living day lights out of us, but you did not. That is reason why we all know that we will miss you, and miss being in the class. We all know that we will all thank about you. We all will miss the good times we all have had in this class room and with all of the ones that are in there. So as you go on through this school as a teacher just remember what we all think of you and if you go to another school still remember all of us in this great class of "72". But you are the one who helped us get through school and we are so glad for you to help us. So keep up all the teaching you have done and don't let anyone give you any B.S. like you did not let us because you know what you are talking about when you tell someone something and you are right every time you say something. So just keep telling all the kids in the class what you think and when they get older they will wish they would have listened to you. So keep it up and don't let anyone get in your way. So we all will come back and see you some time okey. But anyhow thank you so very much for all the help you have gave all of us Seniors. We all wish you and your wife the best of luck through all the years you will be together. Bye Bye.

Signed:
All the Seniors in this class
of "72" in your room.

Good luck Mr. Stewart
with all the class you
will have as you keep teaching.

"72" is the best!!!!

Harold Forwith.
John Galland.
Roger Gekler.
Herman Gray.
Jim Rayburn.
Diane Poth.

We will miss all of you.
So keep smiling for the
whole world knows you CARE!!!!

And also keep smiling for the
whole class of "72" CARES!!!!!

Best wishes through the years
you teach at all the schools
and keep letting the kids know
you are only trying to help them
get through the years at C.H.S.

So keep on saying peace on earth
and just maybe there will be peace
on earth and all the work will be
done.

Chapter 21
Conclusion

 Sometimes, in life, special people enter your life and, for a short time, you become part of them.

Someone who has a winning smile and can make you laugh. I have seen young people walk through hard times and confused times.

If I could live my life over, I would cherish all the memories and relationships I shared with all my past students and staff members that I encountered and thought about the things "God has Blessed Us With!"

I remember my students and past old friends with whom I taught everywhere I go. It makes my heart feel a little lighter and things in my life a little lighter.

MORE PRIME INFORMATION

By:

The Author:

For the Teachers and Parents

Sometimes, in life, special people enter your life and, for a short time, you become part of them.

Someone who has a winning smile and can make you laugh. I have seen young people walk through hard times and confused times.

If I could live my life over, I would cherish all the memories and relationships I shared with all my past students and staff members that I encountered and thought about the things "God has Blessed Us With!"

I remember my students and past old friends with whom I taught everywhere I go. It makes my heart feel a little lighter, things in my life a little lighter, and the world and my smile a little brighter. I am now a much older person, and I realize that sometimes life is important, and so are the students I had while teaching and teachers I remember working with from my past and present. And so, I keep them, their thoughts, and their deeds close in my heart and memory. As a student, you always handed out sunshine the way you were taught, and as a teacher, you handed out sunshine the way you taught!

"To all my past deceased students and Teaching Friends,"

May you all-- R.I.P.

Blessed is the Pure in Heart:

For They Shall See God."

"To My Former Team Members,"

We'll have no more Winning Moments to Celebrate as a team. No more asking for a ride home, and no more of your saying,

"Just a Minute Coach! - - - We're Out of Minutes!"- - Coach Stewart

"HEY TEACH:"

Let's Review a Little More about YOU!

It would be wise to review Chapter 20 and make a few notes about yourself and what you could do to improve your teaching method and the material you're trying to convey to your students.

What do you know about each student? For example, home life, family economy, size, type of parents and abuse in the home. Are they being bullied by others? Many other situations may present themselves if you watch and listen to your students.

FOR NEW SPECIAL NEEDS (EDUCATION) & REGULAR OR INCLUSION, TEACHERS

REVIEW:

How to Handle All Behavioral Disabilities

In Your Classroom.

A few final suggestions from the Coach:

1. Be in your room weeks before school begins to have everything ready when the students enter the door. Have you looked at each student's records and test scores to know what educational grade level each student is comfortable with in reading, reading comprehension, spelling, and math? I tested my students myself at the beginning of each year.

2. Be able to call each student by name and often. Remember all student's names as quickly as possible!

3. What do you know about each student? For example, are they being bullied by others? What's their family life like, or their parents and the size of the family? Are any physical or emotional disabilities displayed in the family by a student or a parent? Have you ever called a student's home to update good news or asked to stop by to give yourself and the parent new insight into their son or daughter? All meetings with parents do not mean bad news. Say something good about the student when you have a chance.

4. If you want to succeed with a student's learning, let the student help set up their I.E.P. and grade each student in class on their ability, not compared to other students. Be familiar with each one's ability; that makes you look like a better teacher and one who's well-liked.

5. Show friendliness to all students and their parents.

6. There is no need to give extra homework as punishment to a Student. "USE THE POINT SYSTEM CHARTS TO HELP CONTROL ALL STUDENTS!" "Stop all art projects until you get the student under control!"

7. If you speak to a student in an unacceptable and intimidating manner, "Then Get the Hell out of Education or Special Education!" No student deserves that type of abuse from a teacher!

8. Encourage the shy student to speak out in private conversation. Conversation.

Here are a few extra tips that may help you with your classroom behavior. Try the Point System. If it works, maybe you'll have one of the best Special Education classes in the State of Ohio, like I did!

Book Title:
"Classroom Climate Control."
Author: Thomas J. Stewart B.S./M.S.

"Coach"

They called me Coach as a nickname because I had been the Head Coach of Three major sports. "Swimming at Col. Crawford High School."

If I could live my life over, I would cherish all the memories and relationships I shared with all my past students and staff members that I encountered and thought about the things "God has Blessed Us With!"

I remember my students and past old friends with whom I taught everywhere I go. It makes my heart feel a little lighter, things in my life a little lighter, and the world and my smile a little brighter. I am now a much older person, and I realize that sometimes life is important, and so are the students I had while teaching and teachers I remember working with from my past and present. And so, I keep them, their thoughts, and their deeds close in my heart and memory. As a student, you always handed out sunshine the way you were taught, and as a teacher, you handed out sunshine the way you taught!

"To all my past deceased students and Teaching Friends," may you all---- R.I.P.

"Blessed is the Pure in Heart:

For They Shall See God."

"To My Former Team Members,"

We'll have no more Winning Moments to Celebrate as a team. No more asking for a ride home, and no more of your saying,

"Just a Minute Coach!

We're Out of Minutes!"

Coach Stewart

"HEY TEACH:"

Let's Review a Little More about YOU!

It would be wise to review Chapter 20 and make a few notes about yourself and what you could do to improve your teaching method and the material you're trying to convey to your students.

What do you know about each student? For example, home life, family economy, size, type of parents and abuse in the home. Are they being bullied by others? Many other situations may present themselves if you watch and listen to your students.

FOR NEW SPECIAL NEEDS (EDUCATION) & REGULAR OR INCLUSION, TEACHERS
REVIEW:
How to Handle All Behavioral Disabilities
In Your Classroom.
A few final suggestions from the Coach:

1. Be in your room weeks before school begins to have everything ready when the students enter the door. Have you looked at each student's records and

test scores to know what educational grade level each student is comfortable with in reading, reading comprehension, spelling, and math? I tested my students myself at the beginning of each year.

2. Be able to call each student by name and often. Remember all student's names as quickly as possible!

3. What do you know about each student? For example, are they being bullied by others? What's their family life like, or their parents and the size of the family? Are any physical or emotional disabilities displayed in the family by a student or a parent? Have you ever called a student's home to update good news or asked to stop by to give yourself and the parent new insight into their son or daughter? All meetings with parents do not mean bad news. Say something good about the student when you have a chance.

4. If you want to succeed with a student's learning, let the student help set up their I.E.P. and grade each student in class on their ability, not compared to other students. Be familiar with each one's ability; that makes you look like a better teacher and one who's well-liked.

Show friendliness to all students and their parents.
There is no need to give extra homework as punishment for a Student.

"USE THE POINT SYSTEM CHARTS TO HELP CONTROL ALL STUDENTS!"
"Stop all art projects until you get the student under Control!"

If you speak to a student in an unacceptable and intimidating manner, "Then Get the Hell out of Education or Special Education!" No student deserves that type of abuse from a teacher!

Encourage the shy student to speak out in private conversation. Conversation.

Here are just a few extra tips that may help you with your classroom behavior. Try the Point System. If it works, then maybe you'll have one of the best Special Education classes in the State of Ohio, like I did!

Book Title: "Classroom Climate Control."

I want to show you a few more pictures of my classroom in 1976. The State of Ohio Council of Exceptional Children called it" one of the top five H.S. classes in Ohio."

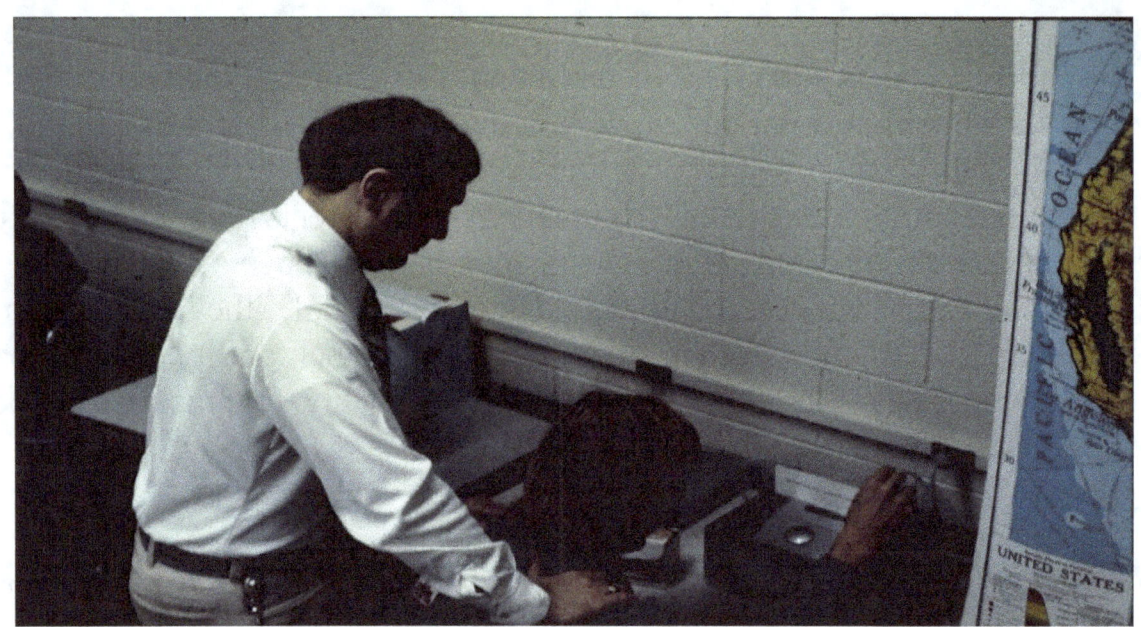

A student is practicing with the guided reader.

Throughout my book, I mention the use of different types of arts and crafts to help control students' behavior problems. Eventually, with the point system and rewards, along with different forms of arts and crafts, you will find a big difference in the overall attitude of the students in your class. They will help each other and work well within group settings.

I taught each student how to use the overhead projector and a sheet of transparency in the printer to make a picture from a black-and-white or color photo. They would trace the image on a small poster board or a piece of wood that they may be able to get from a shop teacher or home, or sometimes if you're in the right area. This person has a scrap wood pile from having a saw-mill on their property; even the Students who have suffered parental abuse will smile when they finish a project and take it home as a gift for their parents. I also trusted a few more of my trustworthy students to use the wood burner to trace their pictures. If students followed the class rules, they became trustworthy and could help others learn. This trust was handed down from year to year. A teacher using this procedure can reduce classroom control by 60—the money we made for the class paid for our class trips and the food.

The Field Trip at Mohican State Park shows Amy and the other students finding biological items in the woods. They were also starving and ready to help me build a campfire for the wieners and other foods we bought for the trip. I always had a trusted driver drive the bus or the van, depending on the number of students I had for the trip.

Renda Thomas beside a classmate doing their scheduled work.

Freshman Basketball team.

Head Coach Cross Country   **_Head Coach Track_**

Mr. William Rall, Guidance Counselor and School Psychologist the P.I.A.T. for each student in class being tested. The students really loved working with the different art projects. The Art was the backbone of each student's learning," Classroom Climate Control!" Group discussion and class reading practice for Filmstrip Presentation at the Greg Poffenbaugh made the Chess Board in the shop class. Greg had Dyslexia but was good with math and how to read blueprints. I found a job for him after school, working for a building Contractor, which is what he became later on in life.

 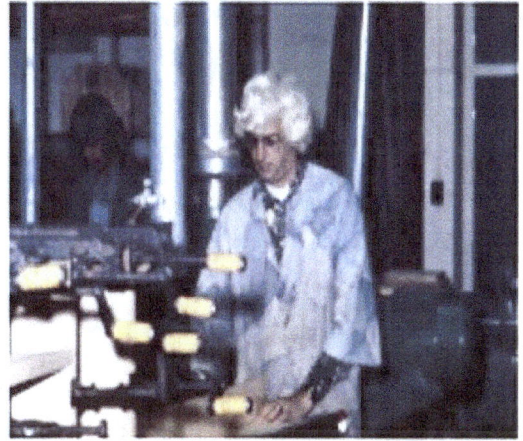

Mr. Bill Klopfenstein Shop

***If anyone wants to tell me that "Full Inclusion" is better than my program?
That would be a challenge I would take you up on!***

Author: Coach Thomas Stewart B.S/M.S.

The reason WE learn: By: "Bev Johns"

As I have pointed out, every writer and reporter has three opinions. In conclusion, I agree with reducing the importance of individual students needing as much testing as the state and federal governments seem to think there should be.

We must do away with the old term "No child left behind!"

We must reinstate the special education classes and provide the money to run them. In addition, teachers need more instructions on how to handle students with behavioral problems. Universities should also require graduate students to do student teaching with students who need behavior control!

We can make the PARENTS more at ease by eliminating the term "FULL INCLUSION" within our public school systems!

I must say that I agree with all the top scholars who have written about "Does Full Inclusion Violate Federal Law?" By: Bev Johns and I also agree with "Socialism in Education."

Written by: Jacob Hornberger

My Book Title agrees with the above writers, and I have the experience to say, "I know because I've lived it and watched the way it's going!"

Final Words for Inclusion and Special Teachers Who Care About Students' Learning

We all have that part of our personality that helps us handle stress resulting from conscious and unconscious forces pursuing our goals—the techniques and skills teachers or parents use.

In my book, you studied a few methods, skills, and programming devised to meet the needs of emotionally disturbed students. The teacher's approach will be to handle disturbed students. The same goes for the parents! However, the transfer of this knowledge for handling less disturbed students will be apparent, as the" DIFFERENCE IS IN DEGREES, NOT IN KIND!" That is important to remember!

*** One of the essential items discussed in my book is student behavioral control—what we want them to aim for!

1. Responsibility

2. Ego Development.

3. Handling of guilt.

4. Handling of Pleasure Activities

5. Immediate gratification

6. Seeking Help.

7. Handling of failure or success.

You have learned that a person's personality is "all they have been, are, and hope to be." It shapes itself out of a person's efforts to achieve an individuality that sets them apart from others and gives them a feeling of worth and value. 179 Are there descriptive criteria for a well-adjusted person? Yes; however, somewhere, we have to draw the line. Finally, the most important of all is to accept and respect themselves and respect those to whom they have control. You have learned that there are techniques that a student lacks. 1. Responsibility. 2. Handling of Pleasure.

3. Handling of Guilt. 4. Handling Failure or Success. 5. Seeking Help. Teachers must be able to handle the above criteria themselves to help students succeed. It won't matter if the student is a "slow learner" or a "Gifted Student;" they will need Social and Emotional guidance. During the testing of young students in lower and higher grades, students must be able to pass different TEST *"Items for Reporting Behavior."*

1. PEER RELATIONS: What is the quality of his give-and-take relationship with others? How does he accept Success? Defeat? Do they dominate others verbally or physically to get their way? Do they take pleasure in provoking others by hitting or teasing others? Is a fearful student dominated and afraid to express their opinion?

2. AUTHORITY LEVEL: Is the student respectful, friendly, and cooperative toward authority, including teachers and parents? Do they continue to test limits? When limits are set, do they become hostile or accept them? Do they resent advice and criticism? Are they hostile toward authority with no apparent cause?

3. SOCIAL AND EMOTIONAL BEHAVIOR: Does the student have low frustration and tolerance levels? Does the student seem depressed a good deal of the time? Have they been brooding, staring, or daydreaming? 180 Do they use threatening ways to get even with others or hold grudges? Can they verbalize their feelings or problems or struggle to express themselves? Does the student present a speech problem at different times? Do they ever show eye-blinking, jerky head and shoulder movements?

4. PERSONALITY DYNAMICS: Are they capable of accepting blame or quick to find reasons why he is right and others are wrong? Do they show guilt or anxiety about their behavior, or are they explosive? Do they have an adequate awareness of right and wrong?

If a teacher can listen to a student's words and tune in on the underlying feelings and emotions, the teacher has a definite advantage. They will be able to anticipate and predict the student's actions before they happen. This, in turn, enables the teacher or parent to manipulate and redirect the student or child's behavior before it is destructive or undesirable. As teachers, we must never forget that all significant behavior, good or bad, adequate or inadequate, is caused by an attempt by the child or student to reduce their tensions and anxieties. Book learning is essential in the function of a school. Still, the main goal is to reverse the failure pattern and character of the lives of the students and children to a successful pattern for each one so they can see themselves as worthwhile and are more than adequate in many ways. Teachers will be intensively involved in a wide range of learning situations for each student.

Experience has taught us that many teachers' or guidance department diagnoses of a given student will vary according to the person making the diagnosis. We must avoid this confusion and ask, "What is the student like?" What are their weaknesses and strengths? How do they relate to other people? What do they think of themselves? Are they bright? What are their academic skills? Do they have any talents?

Based on the answers to all the many questions, as a teacher, I try to set up experiences and activities to enable the students to minimize, remove, or remedy their disabilities. If we find it impossible, we try to help the student adjust despite their defects by teaching him how to substitute using the teacher's skills and knowledge. The teacher must help provide the learning atmosphere for each student day in and day out if the goal of social, emotional, and educational growth is to be attained. All the above statements point us to the following assumptions:

1. Teachers of disturbed students must have a solid foundation in educational methods and a functional understanding of the dynamics of emotional disturbance.
2. Teachers must become "extra good" at reading students at the nonverbal level. This gives a teacher a Head Start in handling students at all learning levels for the slow and the gifted!

In today's world, it is the responsibility of the educator and the parents to develop older students and younger children's capacity to choose and promote proper, socially acceptable behavior that is important for their age group. Teachers should be a significant force in developing students' personalities through their curriculum, planning, activities, and attitudes in the classroom. I have repeated the same comments at different places in my book, hoping that you will remember them and their importance in the classroom and at home. Remember, give students leeway in helping you set standards for behavior and plan class activities.

This means that the "Teacher STAYS in command!" Students should be at the center of our concern, but "Never at the Center of Our Controls!"

   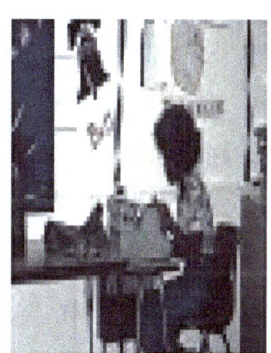

Made by high school students

A successful teacher knows when to throw a change-up, making his regular subject slightly less sour when they feels the temporary student boredom setting in. Sometimes, a break is more desirable than 182 at a particular time. Remember that all students of different age groups will act out when their situation becomes insufficient. The timing of these switches can be a most valuable "planned control" technique. Two H.S. boys made the Wood-burning on heavy art paper by learning to control their behavior to work on their project for Ohio, C.E.C. Bicentennial Convention in 1976: the art display and the "Classroom Climate Control" Project presentation. The above picture was one of the items we displayed at the convention.

Linda

There are many ways that a teacher can help a rowdy student calm down and become a more positive, motivated student in the classroom. A dedicated teacher can inspire parents and students. When students become inspired, they become a positive role model for other students to follow. This will help Teachers become role models for students and connect with the parents of their students in the community. A teacher who cares about their class will find a positive "teacher-student relationship" and have a valued relationship with the parents. A teacher can!!!

"NOTE:" "MOST FOLKS WELL WORTH THE MEMORY HAVE STATUES CARVED IN STONE. BUT TEACHERS MOLD THEIR MONUMENTS IN LIVING SKIN AND BONES!" by "*Margaret O'Rourke.*

You may have gained a few good ideas if you have read this far.

Coach

What would be suitable for all education systems? Think about it. Maybe we should turn our current educational system around by taking the money from the "Federal Special Interest Groups" and restoring our education to the State and Local levels! Then, the Federal Flow-Through Money would have a different system to travel within each school.

Special education students from all parts of the United States have been shifted into regular education classes for over forty-five years or more. However, many present-day educators need more experience handling students with severe behavior in a regular class. Many teachers are becoming frustrated and quitting teaching "Inclusion classes on a High School level."

Many schools around the United States want to offer full-time inclusion, so I have been told! According to the Federal Level of Congress, it is still illegal for a class to go full-time. Inclusion for a specific classroom on a high school level is unlawful.

The money for Special Education classes is now used to support regular courses! Where have the Special Education Teachers gone? They quit! Why? They weren't taught properly how to handle students in grades seven through twelve or how to organize the beginning of the school year to accommodate the actions of severe behavior students and other forms of disability you find in the classrooms. Most Special Education teachers from higher levels of education do not have hands-on methods of learning how to handle students with severe behavior. Most University Professors use a psychological approach to teaching students, which they pass on to future teachers.

WHY IS THAT? Using psychology may sound acceptable when you read about it in a textbook, but more than a textbook is needed in real life. An OLD Expression Is: "Those Who Can Do! Those Who Can't, TEACH!" They added on to that expression, "Those Who Can't Teach, TEACH TEACHERS!" (Professors) Not all university professors teach the same way, using the same material and subject. For instance, I went to Xavier University in Cincinnati, Ohio, and my advisor was the Director of the Longview Children's Unit School in Cincinnati. A teacher in my position learned first-hand how to handle each student, no matter what the student's handicap was.

"Well, teach." Now, read my book and find a few pointers to make yourself and your class proud! I don't care how bad they are! You are the one in charge, not your students! You assign the points awarded for the week. If you're prepared for your class each day and can make it enjoyable for them, then go further and remember what Margaret O'Rourke told you; "You are the one who holds the future of the students in your hands!" Trust me, I know! I have watched them grow from grade seven until now, 2024. Many have retired in their sixties and seventies, raised a family, worked at various places, and are grandparents. How do I know? Hell, Man, I just turned eighty-five (85), and I can still see. What hurts the most is when you find that a few of your former students have died at a young age, and I helped them as long as God wanted me to. After all, he's the one that called me first!

Author: Coach Thomas Stewart B.S./M.S.

P.S.: We all have had disappointments in our lives. My biggest one is not writing my Dissertation for my PhD at Bowling Green State University in Ohio. I did all the classwork, driving almost one and a half hours one-way. But I had been the head coach of three major sports and coached a fourth, along with raising a family, and I did not have the time.

Linda Baldridge   Joe Heffner (R.I.P.)
(Mr. and Mrs. Heffner)

1ST TEAM IN ANY SPORT TO MAKE STATE FINALS.

My Friend, John Tesso of Crestline High School, worked at a department store in Galion, Ohio, and he would bring me leftover supplies to use in my class, and it worked out fine! The severe behavior and unwanted discipline in the room dropped to almost zero in behavior. Notice the bottle on the table. Staining glass and using lead on the bottles was one of our first projects that was sold. That was in 1973.

"Coach" was a nickname they called me at Serena High School in Illinois in 1965.

Col. Crawford, High School in North Robinson, Ohio, 1966 and Crestline High School in Crestline, Ohio, 1967-2000.

HEAD COACH: Trach, Cross-Country, Swimming, Diving and Reserve Basketball

Part of the 70's and 80's class

Track, Swimming, Diving, Cross Country.

Made by the Students in 1976 with the teacher's help

GOD BLESS AMERICA!!

Coach Stewart

Richard Herzog uses his artwork to show his behavior and pride in himself.
He was also one of the main speakers at the C.E.C Convention. "Whitey," spent
most of his life installing the Giant Windmills we see around the United States.

Lonny and John have enough points to sit and study in the soft seats.

Coach Stewart's first Biology class in 1965

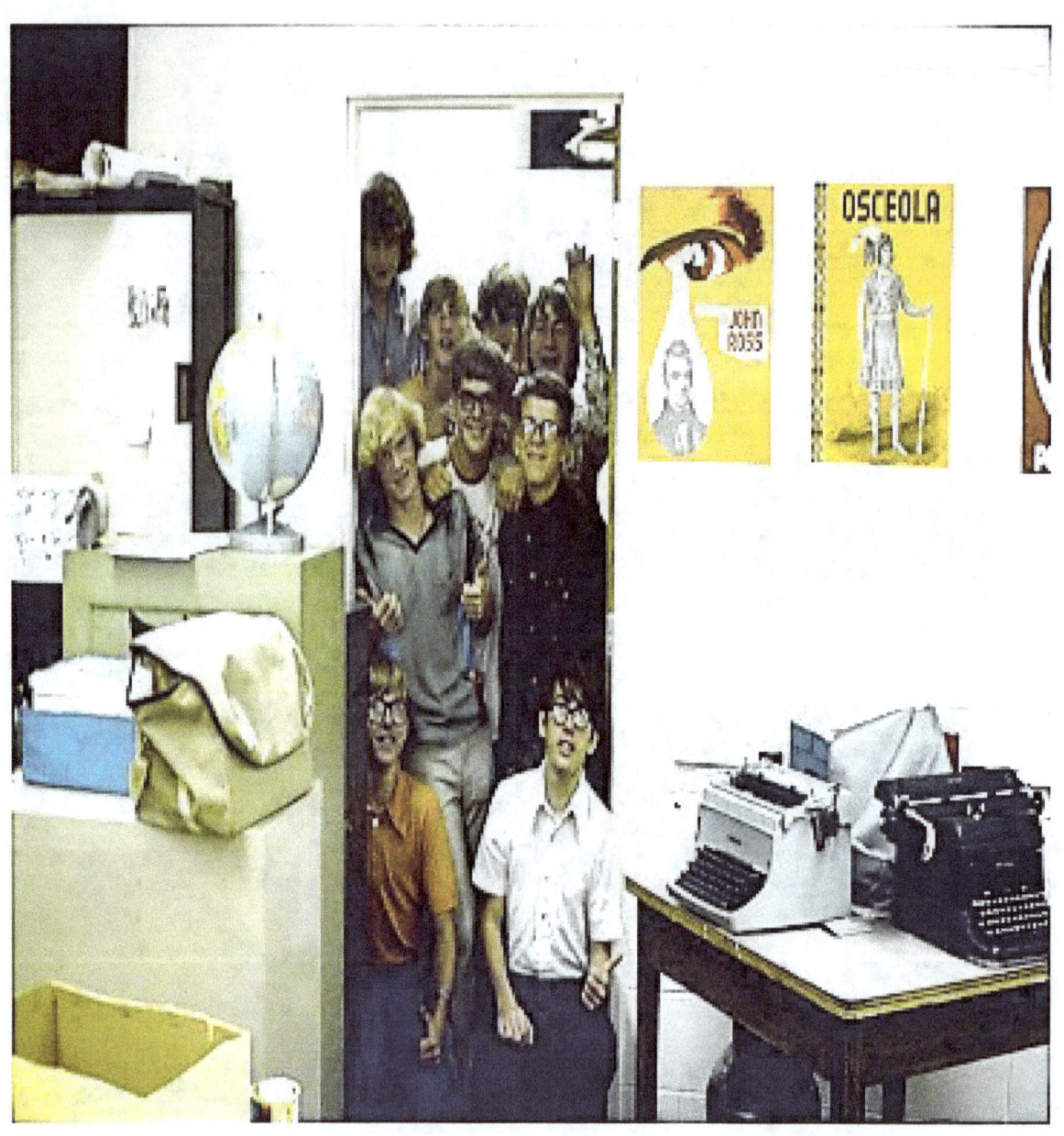

They are a good group of guys who learned to act within the classroom standards to win.

Dinner in Mansfield, Ohio. They ordered what they wanted.

Our room is getting ready for the C.E.C. Bicentennial Convention in 1976. Each student was very proud of their projects and had them shown in the presentation in Cleveland, Ohio

All projects made by students

Our Classroom was made ready by all of the students for the 1976 Bicentennial in Cleveland, Ohio.

Home from the Army 1962

Johnny, Richard, Greg, Jerry
1976 Convention

Coach teaching in science.

Thank you for taking the time to read my book. Coach!

www.ingramcontent.com/pod-product-compliance
Lightning Source LLC
Chambersburg PA
CBHW080126150626
46550CB00017B/2731